IMAGES
of America

MONTGOMERY
VILLAGE

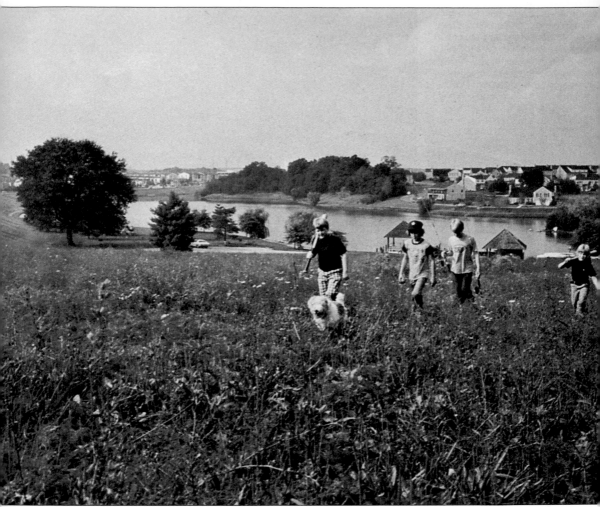

TURNING FARMLAND INTO PEOPLE LAND, DOCKSIDE, 1976. In the early 1960s, a small residential developer, Kettler Brothers Inc. saw an opportunity to build a new town on the old Walker farm. The developer acquired several adjacent farms and began to plan for a large-scale residential community. The Kettler brothers had a vision that the spring-fed stream could become a lake, that the rich soil could give rise to thousands of new trees, and that the growing number of area families could reap the benefits of the good life. The mission for this new community was to be not just a collection of houses in subdivisions but to focus on a new kind of urban development that would provide a total living environment for its residents. (Kettler Brothers Inc.)

ON THE COVER: ENVISIONING THE WAY, EDWARD DESIMON (LEFT) AND CLARENCE KETTLER (RIGHT), 1963. It took extensive planning to turn the existing farmland into a total living environment. DeSimon captured the spirit of the mission when he stated, "We must make a commitment to do a job well done; in doing so we have a true value in ourselves and in the product we produce." (Susan DeSimon and family.)

IMAGES
of America

MONTGOMERY VILLAGE

Montgomery Village Historical Book Committee

ARCADIA
PUBLISHING

Published by Arcadia Publishing
Charleston, South Carolina

Printed in the United States of America

Library of Congress Control Number: 2011926047

For all general information, please contact Arcadia Publishing:
Telephone 843-853-2070
Fax 843-853-0044
E-mail sales@arcadiapublishing.com
For customer service and orders:
Toll-Free 1-888-313-2665

Visit us on the Internet at www.arcadiapublishing.com

*To the Kettler brothers for having the vision to create something
new; to those who worked tirelessly to make their dream a reality;
to those who continue to keep their dream alive; and to the residents
of Montgomery Village who are proud to call the Village home.*

CONTENTS

ACKNOWLEDGMENTS

Unless otherwise noted, all images appear courtesy of the Montgomery Village Foundation (MVF) and are from a donation of materials from Kettler Brothers Inc. Many of the images in the collection were published in the magazine *Living in Montgomery Village Today*, a publication of Kettler Brothers Inc. An invaluable resource for research and photographs for this book were the work of William N. Hurley Jr. and his self-published *Montgomery Village: A New Town* (Van Volumes: Thorndike, MA, 1993). Both the Montgomery County Historical Society and the Gaithersburg Community Museum provided photographs and guidance in preparing this book.

Thank you to the residents of Montgomery Village, past and present, whose treasured memories helped shape this book.

A special thank-you goes to the members of the Historical Book Committee—George Aubin, Gloria Bernero, Pamela Bort, Carolyn Camacho, Mike Conroy, Barbara Fries, Edna Miller, Jennifer Moore, Melanie O'Brien, Marilyn O'Connell, Roslyn Price, and Denise Sheehan—whose time, energy, and hard work are exemplified in every page.

INTRODUCTION

In the mid-1960s, Clarence Kettler asked his brothers Milton and Charles to join him in creating a "new town" in the suburbs, a "planned community" based on a European model that would provide all the elements of the American Dream for its residents. It would be a family-oriented community placing major emphasis on recreation and open space and was to be called Montgomery Village after its location in a county named Montgomery in the heart of Maryland. The word *village* was chosen to promote a small-town feeling in the growing metropolitan area around Washington, DC.

Plans began to take shape when the Kettler brothers acquired farmland adjacent to the city of Gaithersburg, about 20 miles northwest of Washington, DC. The area was booming with employment opportunities but was still relatively rural, with limited housing. Since colonial times, the land had been cleared and cultivated to support small farmers and their families. The Walker family had owned the largest farm in the area since the 1850s. Buildings on some of the surrounding farms dated to the late 18th century. Through a family connection, the Kettler brothers first acquired 412 acres from Ralph and Grover Walker in 1964 and quickly purchased more farms in the area.

The Town Sector Zone, a new zoning category, was created for Montgomery Village. Its purpose was to make possible the building of new towns located far enough from the built-up areas of the Washington metropolitan area to permit a high degree of self-sufficiency as a separate economic and social unit. The full build-out of Montgomery Village has resulted in attractive and desirable neighborhoods, with ample green spaces and preservation of many natural features. The initial plan included 400 acres of green space and a 12-acre man-made lake. Careful planning led to the inclusion of schools, places of worship, a golf course, and the Village Center, along with recreational amenities and walking and bike paths to connect the community. A large regional library, fire station, shopping mall, and other commercial areas are in proximity. The Kettler motto, "Don't simply build on the land—improve upon it," was clear from the beginning.

On October 17, 1966, the Montgomery Village Foundation Inc. (MVF) Articles of Incorporation were recorded with a mission statement setting forth the purpose "to promote the health, safety and welfare of the residents of the community of Montgomery Village." These documents bestowed on the foundation responsibilities that essentially mirror those of a city government. Additional powers are granted to the foundation through declarations of covenants that are included as part of the deed to all residential property within Montgomery Village and associated with all of the 10 homes corporations, 11 condominium associations, and 4 rental apartment complexes. Throughout the Village, there is a variety of housing, with many different architectural styles represented in the different subdivisions. Architectural control was incorporated into the documents in order that design standards and criteria might continue to maintain the harmony of the original design while being continuously updated to permit the use of new materials and design concepts.

The Village was designed to enable its residents to live in community with each other and nature; planning included construction of lakes and ponds and planting of many new trees.

As Montgomery Village grew, farmland became parkland, and saplings became mature trees, earning Montgomery Village a national Tree City award for the past 22 years. Even the Kettler brothers could not have imagined that the land once occupied by farms would evolve into a natural habitat for the many species of birds, animals, and plant life that coexist comfortably with Villagers today.

Lake Whetstone, with its island wildlife, park, paths, boating, and picnic tables, is considered the jewel of the Village. It is a little-known fact that the lake was created by the dam that is the bed of Montgomery Village Avenue in that area. The island, which was once the setting for Fourth of July fireworks, is now a virtual wildlife sanctuary inhabited by herons, cormorants, and other waterfowl and is off-limits to human interference.

The developers wanted to create a family-oriented environment capable of sustaining the recreational needs and interests of residents of all ages. From the beginning, approximately one-fourth of the land was devoted to residents' recreational enjoyment, including more than 35 acres of ponds and lakes, parks, athletic fields, swimming pools, community centers, tennis courts, a golf course, an outdoor amphitheater, a nature center, an indoor aquatic center, and miles of private paths.

In the early years, recreational possibilities relied heavily on Montgomery County programs held in Village community centers. Gradually, the foundation expanded its own offerings of user-fee classes for all ages, including dance, art, sports, tennis, swim lessons, preschool programs, summer camps, adult aerobics, yoga, and much more. Village-wide special events include the annual Fourth of July celebration; the Art, Craft and Photography Show; seasonal celebrations such as the annual Fall Festival; Halloween programs for children; a Christmas-tree lighting, and others.

Today, Montgomery Village has more than 40,000 residents, and it celebrates its 45th anniversary in the fall of 2011. As Montgomery Village has grown, farms have been replaced by well-manicured residential areas and mature trees. The foundation has expanded its ownership of public land, which now totals more than 330 acres, for the benefit of all residents and owns and operates 7 pools, 22 tennis courts, 4 community centers, 18 recreation and park areas, a natural amphitheater, and a nature center. Volunteer groups are working to plan for new amenities and enhancements to existing facilities to move the Village forward to meet the needs and desires of future generations.

Active swim teams, the annual Fourth of July parade and celebration, our popular community band, and programs and special events for all ages continue to play an integral role in the vibrant life of Village residents. Photographs of many of these events, along with historic and anecdotal photographs representing the history of our community, are included in this book and bear witness to the developers' long-advertised motto for the Village, "Living the Good Life."

Montgomery Village takes pride in its active community volunteers, premier parks, recreation and community facilities, and a commitment not only to maintain but also to enhance the natural environment and coexist with our many species of wildlife. Although the Village is no longer a new town, it continues to serve as an admirable and viable model for communities everywhere. Today, Montgomery Village still embodies the Kettler brothers' vision: "people living life to its fullest potential, in an environment that is supporting, enriching, alive . . . that is what we hope to bring to the community. That is what our efforts are all about."

One

THE LAND

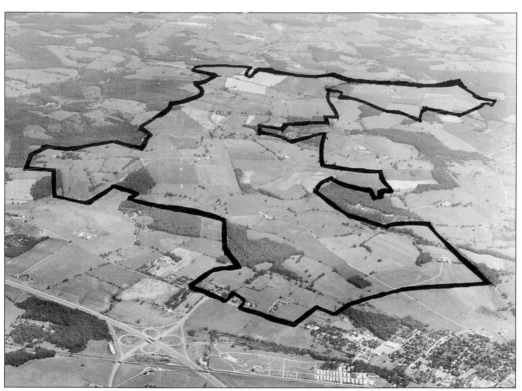

FUTURE SITE OF A NEW TOWN, C. 1964. Montgomery Village, Maryland, would be built on more than 2,500 acres of individual farms just north of Gaithersburg, Maryland (seen at the bottom right). The cloverleaf interchange to Interstate 70 South (now I-270) can be seen on the lower left. Since the late 18th century, this land had supported small farmers and remained relatively unchanged.

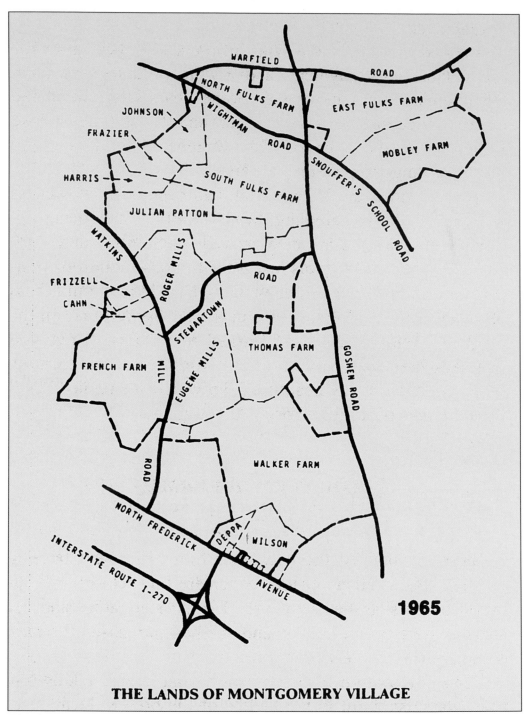

THE LANDS OF MONTGOMERY VILLAGE

THE ORIGINAL FARMS, 1965. In his book detailing the history of Montgomery Village, William N. Hurley Jr. created this map outlining and naming the original farms that covered the land. Many of these farmers gave their names as well as their lands to the new community, such as Thomas Choice, Millrace, Patton Ridge, Frenchton Place, and many others. (William N. Hurley Jr., *Montgomery Village: A New Town.*)

DEED TO THE WALKER FARM, 1849. In October 1849, Nathan J. Walker purchased a small farm north of Gaithersburg, Maryland, for the sum of $900 "current money." Since colonial times, the tracts of land where a small creek, called Whetstone Run, passed through the property had been known as Crabb's Fortress and Lost Knife. (Montgomery County Historical Society.)

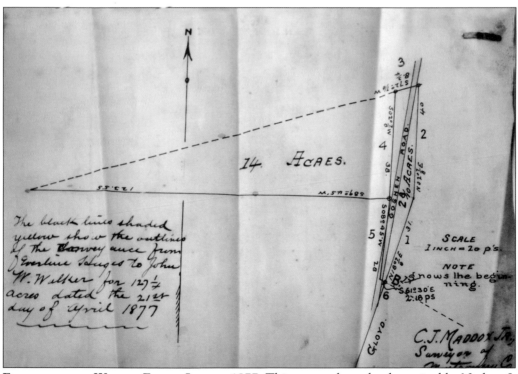

EXPANDING THE WALKER FAMILY LANDS, 1877. This survey shows land acquired by Nathan J. Walker's eldest son, John Wesley Walker, in 1877. "Wes" Walker served as mayor of Gaithersburg from 1906 to 1908 and again from 1918 to 1924. Goshen Road, on the eastern edge of the survey (at the right side of the photograph), bisected the family farm. (Montgomery County Historical Society.)

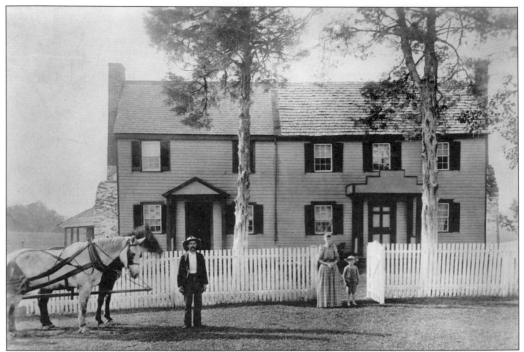

THE NATHAN J. WALKER HOME, C. 1900. Originally a log cabin, the Walker farmhouse expanded and grew with the family. Nathan J. Walker and his wife, Eveline King Walker, raised 11 children here. Walker was a prominent member of the Grace Methodist Church, located at Route 355 and Walker Avenue and built in 1905. A stained glass window there commemorates his service to the congregation. (Ralph Walker, Gloria Walker Keesee, and Gaithersburg Community Museum.)

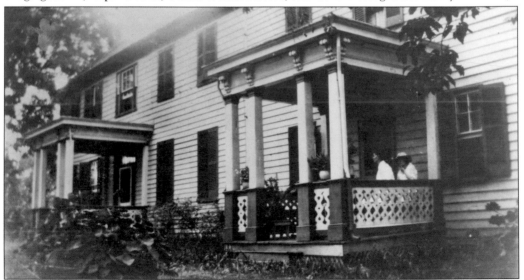

THE NATHAN J. WALKER HOME, C. 1910. In the early 20th century, prominent "twin" porches were added to the Walker family home. Fifty years later, this one house would make way for thousands of new residences. Today, this same land is home to Walker's Choice, Cider Mill, Horizon Run, Christopher Court, Dockside, Nathan's Hill, and Millrace. (Montgomery County Historical Society.)

RALPH WALKER AND FAIR OAK MISS RUE. McKendree Walker, youngest son of Nathan and Eveline Walker, took over the farm from his father. By the mid-20th century, he and his two sons, Ralph and Grover Walker, had developed an outstanding herd of Holstein-Friesian cattle and gained international recognition for innovative techniques in farming. (Ralph Walker, Gloria Walker Keesee, and Gaithersburg Community Museum.)

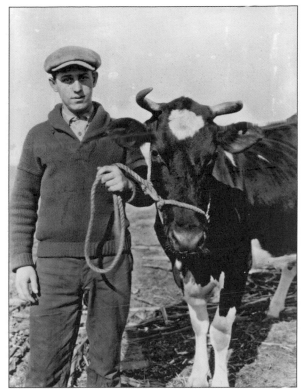

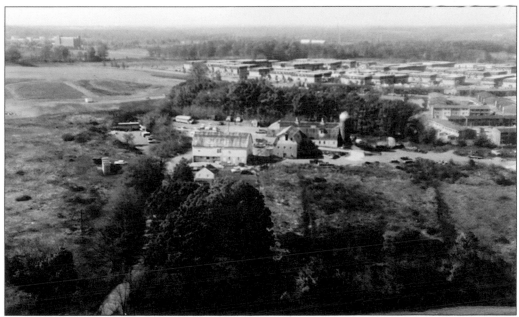

ROLLING KNOLL, THE WALKER FARM, 1969. Grover and Ralph Walker sold their historic family farm in 1961 to Milton Kettler (married to their niece, Barbara Walker) for construction of a new town, Montgomery Village, Maryland. After construction began, Grover Walker and his wife, Marian, remained on a portion of the old farm near Goshen Road, seen in the middle of the photograph with Cider Mill Apartments in the background.

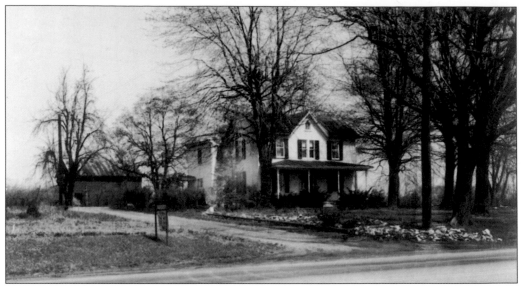

THE DEPPA FARMHOUSE. The farmhouse of James Walter Deppa sat near what is today the Holiday Inn on Route 355. At one time, it was one of the last houses on the north end of Gaithersburg, surrounded by rural farmland. Deppa operated Country Gardens Nursery on this land, and after selling the farm for Montgomery Village, he consulted on tree planting during the construction of the new community.

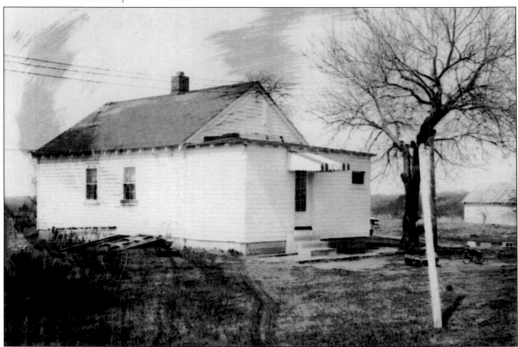

WILSON TENANT HOUSE. James "Pop" Wilson owned a large farm with a small stream running through it near today's Lakeforest Mall. The farm was subdivided and sold many years prior to the building of Montgomery Village. When one of those subsequent owners, a Mrs. Odend'hal, sold her land for Montgomery Village, she requested her family name be used for the new street to run through her property.

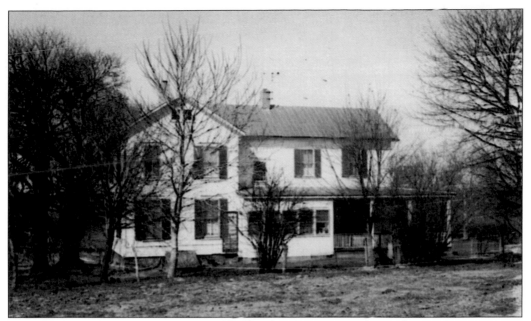

EUGENE MILLS FARMHOUSE. Eugene and his brother, Roger, owned two adjacent farms running along Watkins Mill Road. Today, these lands are home to the Village Center, Heron's Cove, Center Court, Center Stage, Clubside, and part of the golf course. As a condition of the sale, the Mills brothers required that both farms be purchased and asked the developers to contract for them two new adjoining farms in Frederick County.

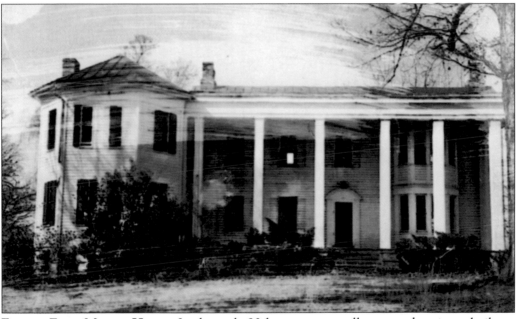

FRENCH FARM MANOR HOUSE. In the early 20th century, a well-respected engineer built an opulent manor house west of Watkins Mill Road. The stately home sat far back from the road, near what is today the Ridges of Stedwick. When developers purchased the land for Montgomery Village in 1964, the home had been deserted and was occupied by squatters who used the grand old staircase for firewood.

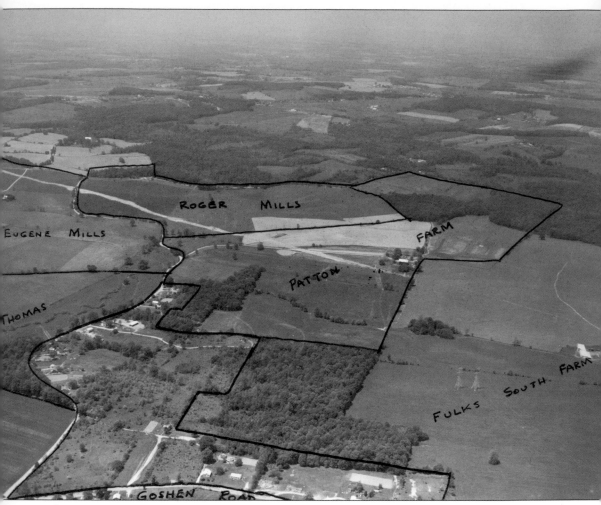

STEWARTOWN, LOOKING WEST FROM GOSHEN ROAD. The unlabeled section of this photograph (lower center) was land originally sold or gifted to former slaves following the Civil War. In 1879, Charles H. Stewart purchased three acres in this area, and in 1902, Richard H. Stewart purchased six acres. Both men, of unknown relation to each other, gave their names to the community that developed there. In 1910, Stewartown Road was built to connect Watkins Mill and Goshen Roads. In the late 1960s, during the development of Montgomery Village, the Stewartown community remained intact even though the developers purchased surrounding farms. The community did not escape the growth of development in the area, and by the late 1970s, Stewartown had become a modern townhome development similar to, but separate from, Montgomery Village. Today, the surrounding farms are home to Thomas Choice, Maryland Place, Highfield, Greentee, Partridge Place, and parts of the golf course.

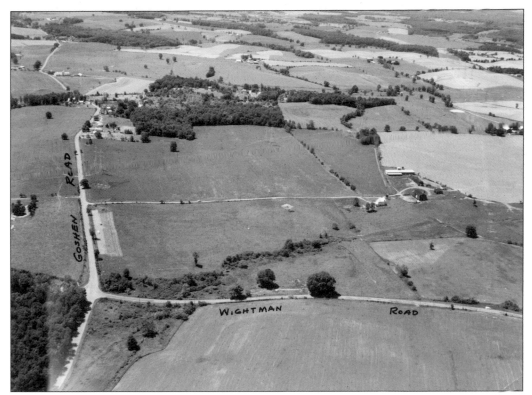

INTERSECTION OF WIGHTMAN AND GOSHEN ROADS. Called Williams Range in the original land grant, this property was purchased in 1762 by the Dorsey family, whose descendants continued to farm it until 1925. The stone house built in the late 1700s can be seen at the end of the lane running through the middle of the photograph. Today, this land is home to the Goshen Shopping Plaza as well as Partridge Place, Greentee, Arrowhead, and Overlea.

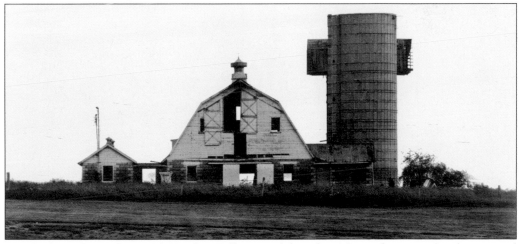

THE BARN AT FULKS FARM. McKendree Fulks owned three large farms that are today the east and north portion of Montgomery Village, including a street named in his family's honor (Fulks Farm Road). As a successful farmer and entrepreneur, Fulks operated multiple businesses, including Farmer Fulks Greenhouses on Woodfield Road. After selling his farmland, Fulks and his wife kept an apartment at the new Walker House, near his native land.

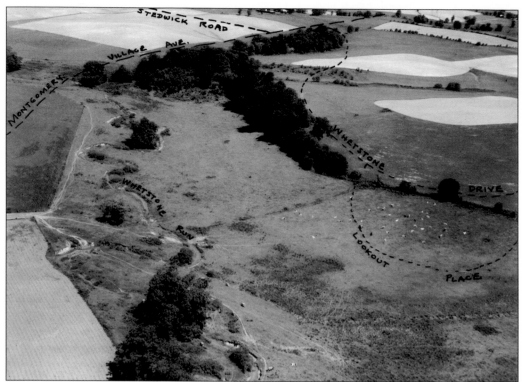

SITE OF LAKE WHETSTONE, C. 1965. Since colonial times, a small stream called Whetstone Run had served as the main geographical feature of this land. Originating nearby in Washington Grove, the feeding spring was said to be capped by a large sharpening stone or whetstone. To create lakes for the new community, developers dammed several small streams including Whetstone Run, which then gave its name to the largest lake.

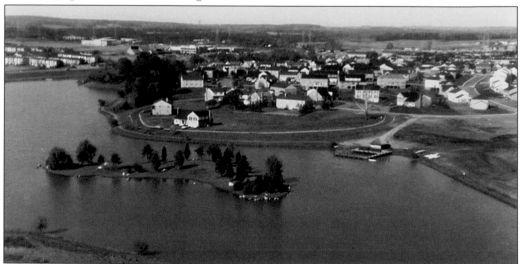

LAKE WHETSTONE, C. 1968. The lake became a central feature of the new community, created by a dam that supports Montgomery Village Avenue. During construction, developers used soil excavated from the land to create the island and planted trees there before allowing the lake to fill. Lake Whetstone has a surface area of about 27 acres and is about 19 feet deep.

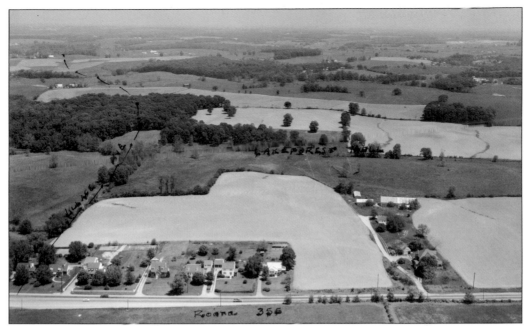

FREDERICK AVENUE LOOKING EAST, 1964. Frederick Avenue (today Route 355) originated as a Native American trail and connected the cities of Frederick and Georgetown in the late 1700s. Benjamin Gaither gave his name to the railroad town that developed along this route in the 1800s. Gaithersburg remained relatively rural throughout the early 1900s, until businesses and housing developments turned the community into a true suburb of Washington, DC.

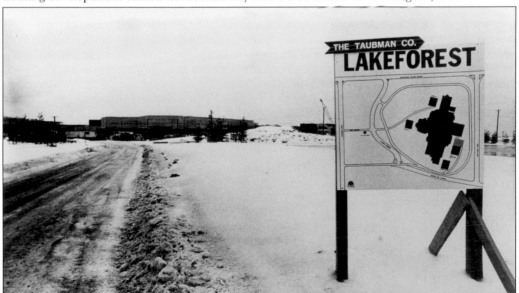

LAKEFOREST MALL, 1976. On the cleared farmland planned to be home to a regional shopping center, the developers of Montgomery Village created a small lake and planted a cluster of trees in 1969. When construction began on the center six years later, local citizens protested the destruction of the man-made Lake Walker and small forest. The appropriately named Lakeforest Mall opened in 1978 and was at the time the largest indoor mall in the United States, according to www.gaithersburghistory.com. (Montgomery County Historical Society.)

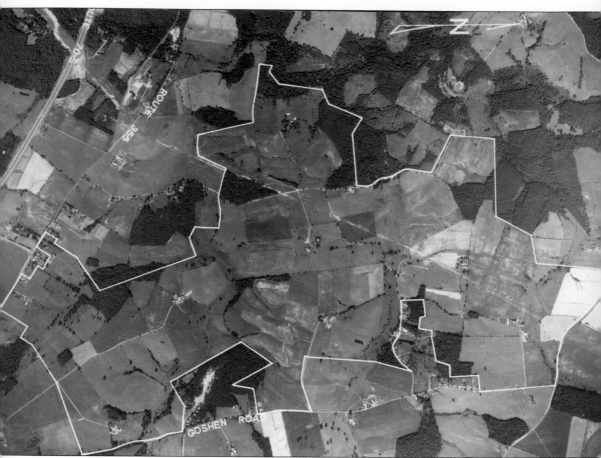

THE LAND BEFORE CONSTRUCTION BEGAN, C. 1964. Beginning at Route 355 near the cloverleaf entrance to Interstate 270, this photograph shows the outline of what would become Montgomery Village (minus the later additions of the North and East Village, beyond Wightman Road at the top of the photograph). Since colonial times, this land supported small farmers who benefited from the fruits of the rich soil. These farms were home to prominent members of the local community like Gaithersburg mayor John "Wes" Walker and successful entrepreneurs like McKendree Fulks. Along with people, this land provided a home to thousands of native plants and animals, including over 20 species of birds identified as indigenous to the area. By the mid-1960s, it nurtured an innovative idea in urban development, a new planned community. This land, which had remained relatively unaltered since the 1800s, underwent rapid change as construction began on the new community of Montgomery Village.

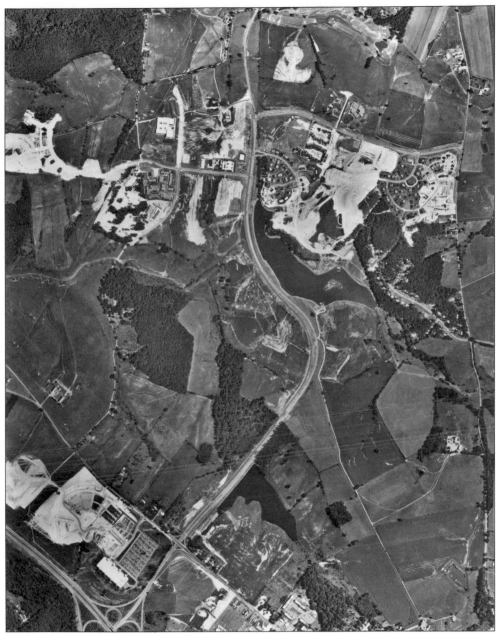

THE LAND AFTER CONSTRUCTION BEGAN, C. 1969. Beginning at the cloverleaf entrance to Interstate 270 in the bottom left, Montgomery Village Avenue was the main thoroughfare for the community (shown through the center of the photograph). Lake Whetstone can be seen just after the curve of the main road, with a few houses in the Lakeside neighborhood built nearby. To the left, some of the new roads built for the Stedwick neighborhood and land cleared for construction are visible. To the right, Centerway Road connects Montgomery Village Avenue to Goshen Road on the far right. Along Centerway, the U-shaped Courts of Whetstone can be seen at one end and Whetstone Circle in the Goshenside neighborhood on the other end. The developers strove to preserve and enhance the natural environment wherever possible, creating open spaces, lakes, and parks within all of the new neighborhoods.

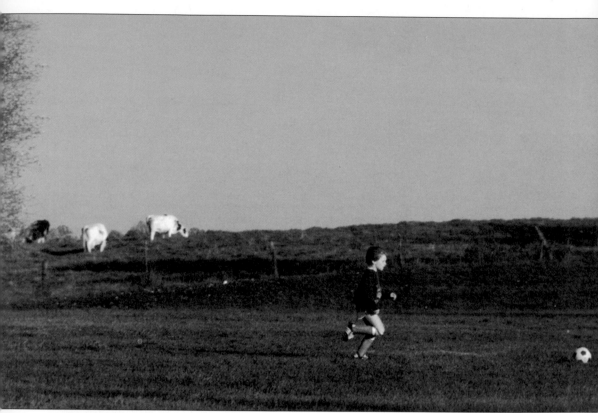

TURNING FARMLAND INTO PEOPLE LAND. In the early 1960s, small residential developer Kettler Brothers Inc. saw an opportunity to develop a new town on farmland owned by the family of Milton Kettler's wife, Barbara Walker Kettler. The company acquired several adjacent farms north of the rapidly growing city of Gaithersburg and began to plan for a large-scale residential community. The Kettler brothers set forth a mission for this new community to be more than just a collection of houses in subdivisions; they hoped to make a new kind of urban development that would provide a total living environment for its residents.

Two

VISION AND MISSION

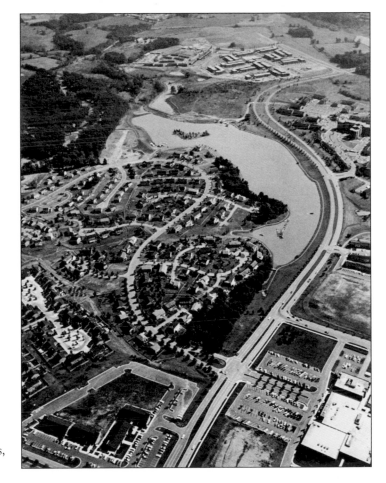

A VISION REALIZED, MONTGOMERY VILLAGE, MARYLAND, C. 1972. Clarence Kettler and his brothers, Milton and Charles, collaborated to create an "American Dream" community that would embody a total way of life in the midst of parklike settings. This planned community was different from other suburban towns emerging at the time, as it provided for schools, places of worship, recreation, shopping, medical services, and cultural life.

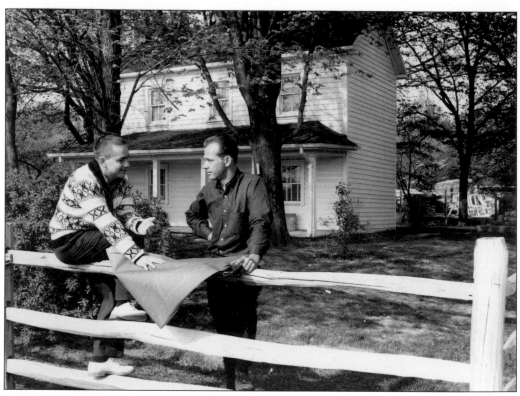

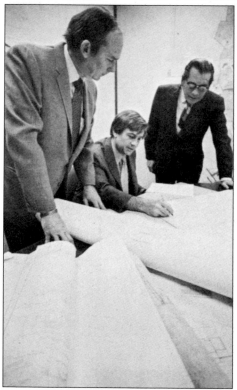

ENVISIONING THE WAY, CLARENCE KETTLER (LEFT) AND EDWARD DESIMON, 1963. Following graduation form the University of Michigan in 1951, Clarence Kettler, the youngest member of the family, temporarily handled family property management. He had studied architecture and design and shortly thereafter decided to become a home builder, persuaded his brothers to join him, and had the opportunity to put his creativity to work designing new ways for people to live. Ed DeSimon was responsible for community site grading and utility construction, later became manager of land development, and eventually retired as senior vice president (Susan DeSimon and family.)

KETTLER BROTHERS INC., SOLE DEVELOPERS AND BUILDERS OF MONTGOMERY VILLAGE, C. 1972. The hands-on approach of the family company created a new town that embodied the company philosophy: "Value in development is the result of total effort. It is the doing of many things better rather than just doing one thing well, that makes the difference between true value which is lasting and apparent value which is superficial."

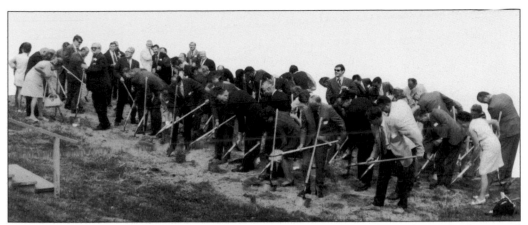

GROUND-BREAKING, FEBRUARY 28, 1966. The Montgomery County Council gave final approval in 1965 to the biggest rezoning application in its history. The initial 1,767 acres of Montgomery Village included 557 acres of open space. The articles of incorporation, filed the same year, envisioned the new town having "a high degree of self sufficiency and independent existence" with an expected population of more than 30,000 people.

A SYMBOL FOR MONTGOMERY VILLAGE, ADOPTED IN 1966. The widely recognized logo of Montgomery Village was derived from an ancient symbol of friendship representing two people clasping hands in peace and harmony. Months of research led Kettler Brothers Inc. to select this image, demonstrating the level of meticulous planning that went into every aspect of the new community.

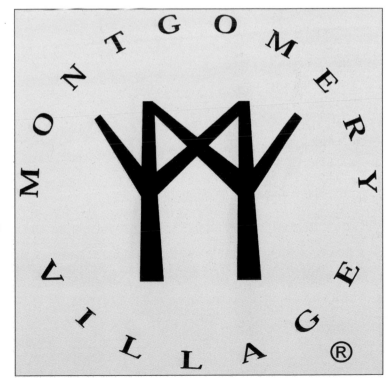

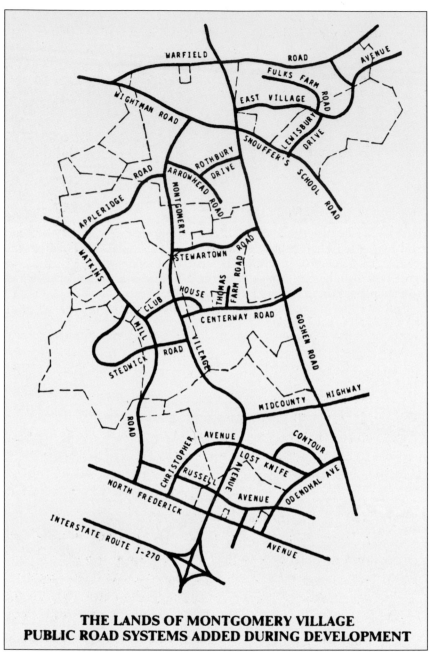

**THE LANDS OF MONTGOMERY VILLAGE
PUBLIC ROAD SYSTEMS ADDED DURING DEVELOPMENT**

NEW ROADS OF MONTGOMERY VILLAGE. Planning the new community required dividing the original farmland into new neighborhoods. The dotted lines on this map show the original farms (seen on page 10). A great deal of thought was given to the naming of the communities and the streets within them. Besides using names from the farms, Kettler Brothers Inc. used original deeds dating back to colonial times, such as Williams Range, Lost Knife, and Dorsey's Regard for the new community. The company also turned to the diary of a Montgomery County resident, Roger Brooke Farquar, written in the late 1800s. In the Whetstone neighborhood, street names were taken from a place or event found in the diary and arranged in alphabetical order. (William N. Hurley Jr., *Montgomery Village: A New Town.*)

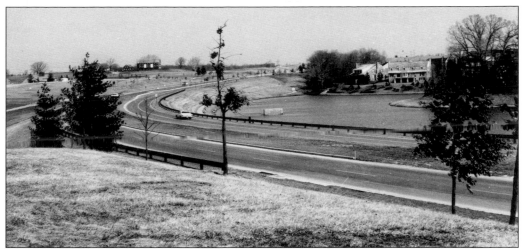

MONTGOMERY VILLAGE AVENUE, C. 1968. The sweeping avenue was designed as a focal point and main artery through the community. After three days considering alternatives for the road, Clarence Kettler decided that the two lanes should be at different levels so that the lake could be seen clearly from either direction. In the upper left, the Eugene Mills barn can be seen where the Village Mall would one day stand.

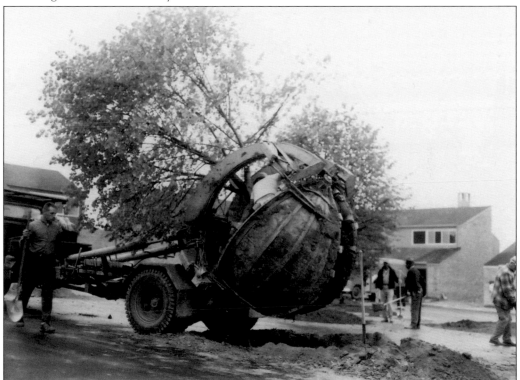

PLANTING MATURE TREES ON CLEARED FARMLAND, C. 1968. Kettler Brothers Inc. placed an order for 10,000 pin oak trees and purchased an unusual tree-moving machine, one of the first to be found on the East Coast. Lady Bird Johnson even enlisted the unique piece of equipment during a beautification project in Washington, DC. Over the years, the Kettler brothers planted their own white pine tree farms for eventual use in the community.

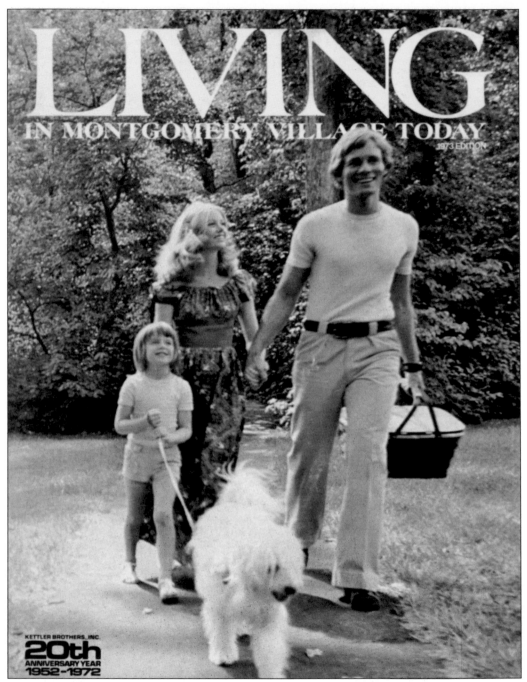

LIVING IN MONTGOMERY VILLAGE TODAY, 1973. As prospective buyers came to investigate the new town, a full-color magazine extolled the amenities of the new community. The photographs and descriptions showed the benefits of life in Montgomery Village and hinted at plans for the future. It exemplified the motto that had driven the planning process, "When you get there, there's a there there." Montgomery Village was an example of how haphazard tract development could be avoided in the sprawling suburbs of Washington, DC.

LAKE WHETSTONE, C. 1974. The lake was designed to set a tone of spaciousness and to provide a welcoming entry to Montgomery Village. It also served as part of an elaborate storm water management system. The 19-foot-deep lake was built with gradually sloping sides for safety and was deep enough to control the growth of algae. During development, it was drained and refilled to meet exacting specifications.

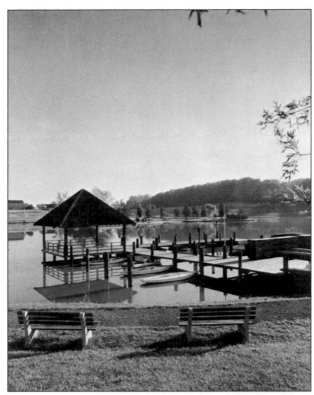

THE PROFESSIONAL CENTER, 1974. The center, conveniently located in the middle of the Village, was part of the vision from the beginning. It provided for the medical and health needs of the new town. Two-story contemporary buildings were clustered around a center garden plaza with covered walkways and ramps. The center provided not only services but also employment for many residents.

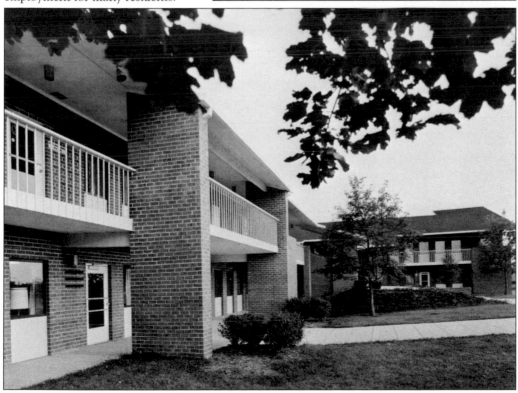

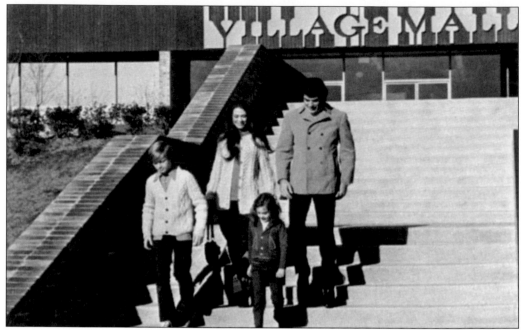

THE VILLAGE MALL, C. 1972. To provide the convenience of downtown within minutes of each home, Kettler Brothers Inc. planned a central shopping center on the main avenue. The mall initially housed 18 shops and boutiques, a movie theater, and additional shops, and an adjacent eatery called the Village Quarter came later.

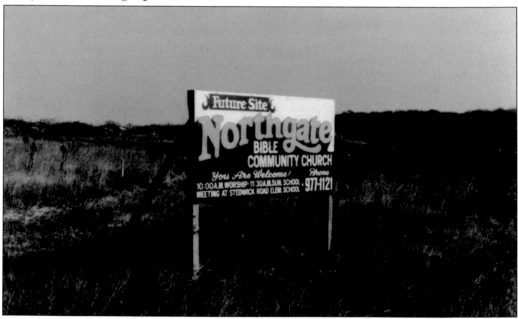

PLANNING FOR PLACES OF WORSHIP, 1972. Central to the plan for the community were multiple sites for places of worship. While raising funds and constructing new buildings, some congregations met in local schools. Initially, the sites were sold to individual congregations, but later tracts were donated by Kettler Brothers Inc., and gratuities were paid to those who previously had paid for their sites. (Lynda Switzer.)

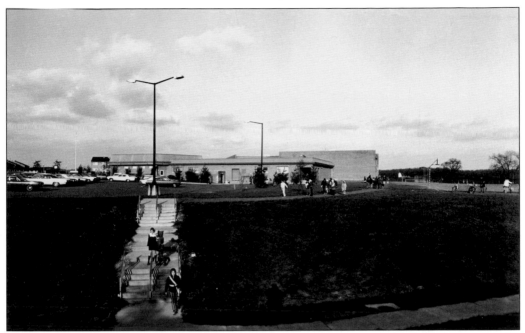

WHETSTONE ELEMENTARY SCHOOL, 1968. The zoning ordinance required that public school sites be identified in the Land Use Plan. The original plans for Montgomery Village determined potential sites for two junior high schools and seven elementary schools. As development progressed and needs changed, adjustments were made to the locations and number of schools.

COMMUTERS BOARD BUS TO WASHINGTON, DC, c. 1973. Direct bus service from the Village Mall to Washington, DC, was available before the Metro system was completed. There were, however, many employment opportunities closer to Montgomery Village. Located at the heart of the 70-S corridor, now I-270, nearby employers included Fairchild Industries, IBM, the Atomic Energy Commission, Bechtel, National Geographic, and the National Bureau of Standards.

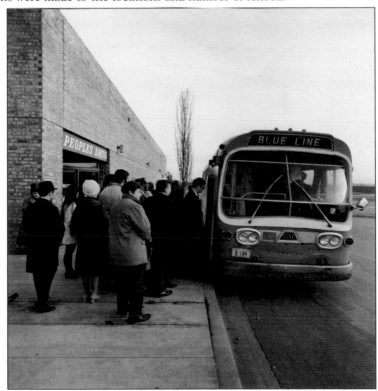

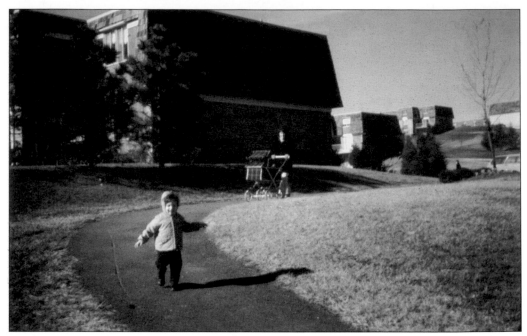

WINDING PATHS AND BIKE TRAILS, 1973. The paved paths were a signature feature in the layout and original design of Montgomery Village. Interwoven throughout the community, the paths safely connect neighborhoods to each other and to community facilities. Residents can enjoy a nature walk by just stepping out the door. (Roslyn Price.)

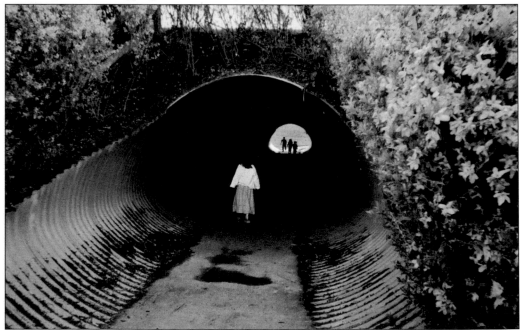

PEDESTRIAN TUNNEL. The small-town feeling was carried throughout the community by the pedestrian tunnels that enabled residents to walk to schools, parks, and shopping areas without crossing busy streets. Safety for pedestrians was a consideration during all aspects of planning. (Lynda Switzer.)

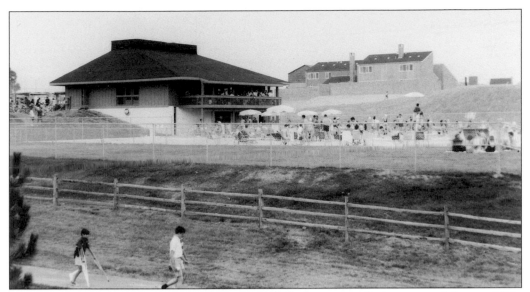

WHETSTONE COMMUNITY CENTER, SUMMER 1968. In keeping with the vision of the good life, the plan for Montgomery Village included community recreation centers within walking distance of every home. Each center provided a pool, tennis courts, and play areas as well as indoor space for meetings and classes.

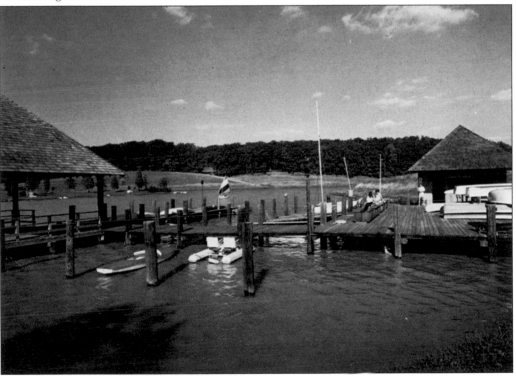

BOAT DOCK AT LAKE WHETSTONE. Planning for recreation was evident from the beginning. Lake Whetstone had two boating docks and hosted waterfront activities. The shores were surrounded by a walking path, benches, and picnic tables. The lake was stocked with several hundred fingerling bass and sunfish to accommodate fishermen both young and old.

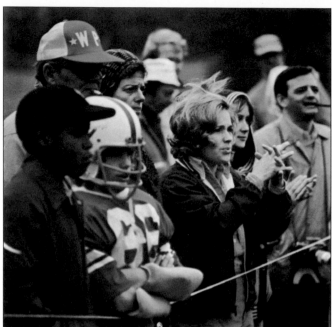

ORGANIZED SPORTS, C. 1977. The many parks and ball fields encouraged the growth of organized team sports and a sense of community. The Kettler brothers envisioned "people living life to its fullest potential, in an environment that is supporting, enriching, alive."

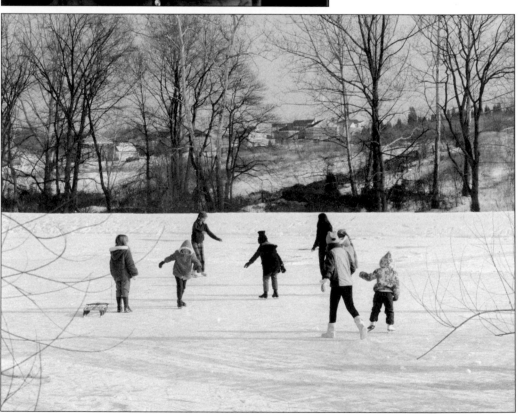

SKATERS ENJOY THE ICE, C. 1972. Even in the winter, the open spaces of Montgomery Village provided ample opportunity to enjoy the outdoors in the parklike setting. Along with lakes and ponds, a 150-acre golf course was planned to provide a manicured, open landscape all year-round.

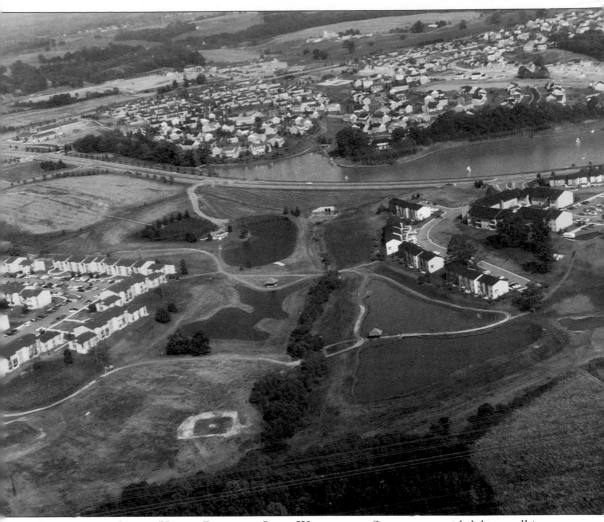

OVERLOOKING SOUTH VALLEY PARK AND LAKE WHETSTONE. Open spaces with lakes, walking paths, and parks were central to the planning of Montgomery Village. Individual communities, each with its own architectural style, were blended into a total environment. Whatever type of home residents wanted—whether rental, single-family, or townhouse—and whatever style—traditional or contemporary, Kettler Brothers Inc. had something to offer. Different communities were designed to reflect the styles and needs of families.

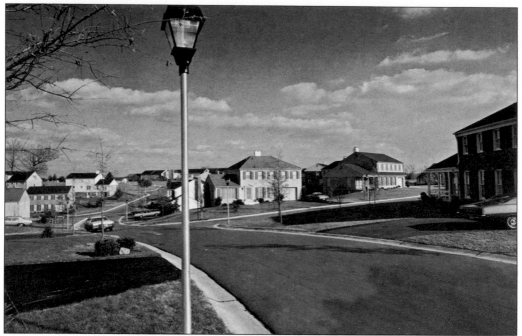

TRADITIONAL SINGLE-FAMILY HOMES. Lakeside of Whetstone was the first community to be developed. It featured five- and six-bedroom single-family homes. The landscaping followed the contours of Lake Whetstone and set the environmental tone for future communities.

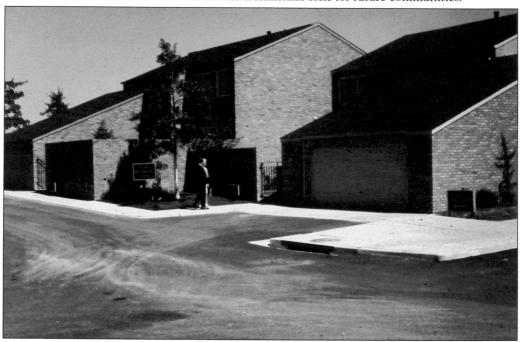

SINGLE-FAMILY GARDEN LIVING. The award-winning California Contemporary–style Courts of Whetstone homes introduced the concept of zero-lot-line development in the Washington area. They blended contemporary architecture with the age-old concept of court garden living. (Lynda Switzer.)

LARGE COLONIAL TOWNHOUSES. In the mid-1960s, Montgomery Village introduced large-scale townhouses to Montgomery County, where they were rare, probably due to a lack of suitable zoning. A social stigma connected with the row house or townhouse concept persisted as a holdover from inner-city developments. The large Colonial-style townhouses of Montgomery Village changed that perception. They were spacious 30-foot-wide townhomes with walled gardens and garages.

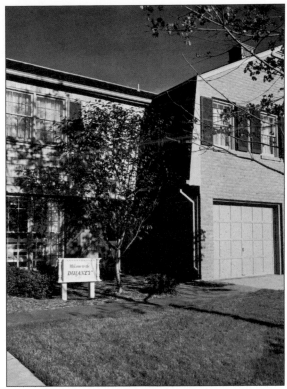

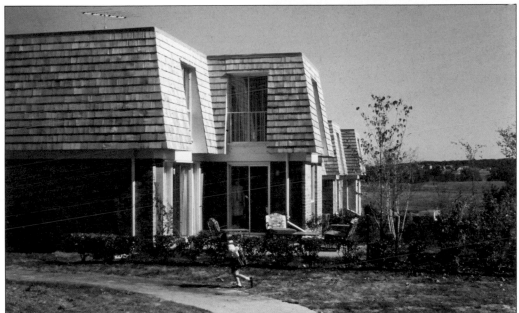

CONTEMPORARY TOWNHOUSES. The Clusters of Stedwick deviated from the traditional Colonial style. The shake mansard roofs, arched entrances, and enclosed garages surrounded an open interior space that was appealing to young families and available at a lower cost than single-family homes. The communities of Stedwick derived their name from an old English term meaning meadow, or land that was once a dairy farm. (Lynda Switzer.)

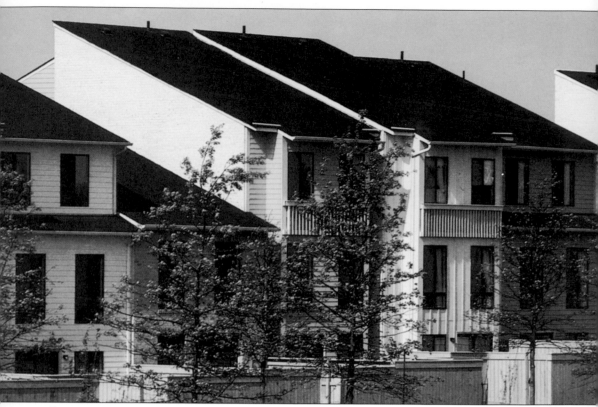

BACK-TO-BACK TOWNHOUSES. The modern-style Clubside pioneered the concept of a back-to-back townhouse design, produced primarily to provide housing at lower costs for first-time purchasers.

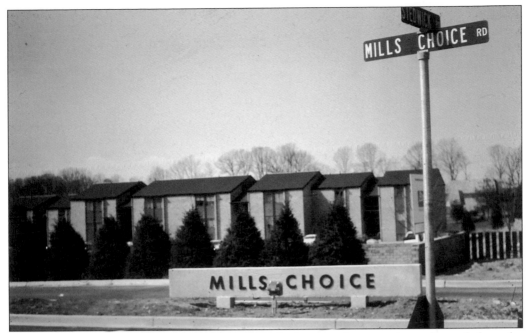

RENTAL GARDEN APARTMENTS. Mills Choice was the first rental community and rounded out the full spectrum of living types available to prospective residents. The word *choice* is an old English term associated with rental properties. Kettler Brothers Inc. combined that idea with the names of early landowners when choosing community names. (Lynda Switzer.)

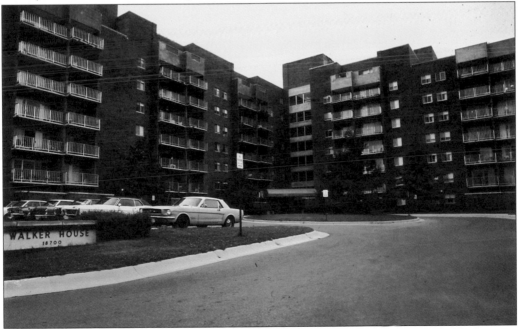

HIGH-RISE APARTMENTS. Walker House was designed as an eight-story apartment building in the center of the Walkers Choice community. This all-rental community offered garden-style and mid-rise apartments as well as townhouses. Located adjacent to South Valley Park, the community was designed to be convenient to the Village Mall. (Lynda Switzer.)

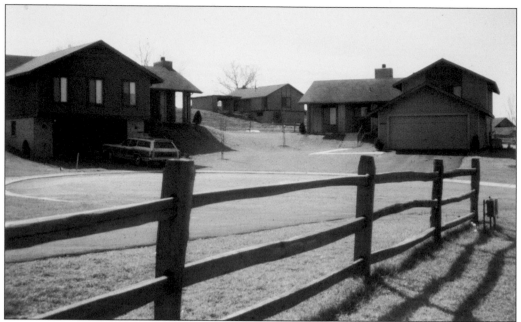

DIVERSITY OF STYLE, CONTINUITY OF NEIGHBORHOODS. The developers planned variety and choice in architectural styles with homes situated in pleasing clusters surrounded by open space that created a park-like setting. The California Contemporary homes of The Heights blended into the environment through use of natural, earthy materials. By contrast, the stately colonials of Whetstone echoed traditional-style houses but still melded with the natural landscape through the colors and materials used in construction. Regardless of housing styles, the rustic split-rail fencing added a rural feeling and provided a sense of continuity throughout the communities. (Above, Jerrold Ward; below, Lynda Switzer.)

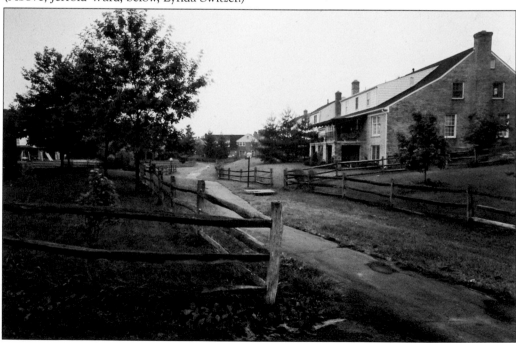

Three

COMMUNITY BEGINNINGS

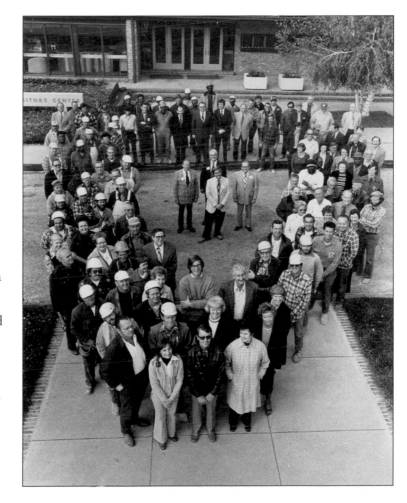

KETTLER BROTHERS INC. Implementing the extensive plan for Montgomery Village was big business, but one with heart. In 1966, Kettler Brothers Inc. held a meeting with all business partners from attorneys to plumbers and invited the small businesses to grow and expand with the new community. Building Montgomery Village would require 30,000 toilets, 80,000 faucets, 12,000 complete kitchens, hundreds of acres of roofing, over 100,000 doors, and millions of bricks. (George Aubin.)

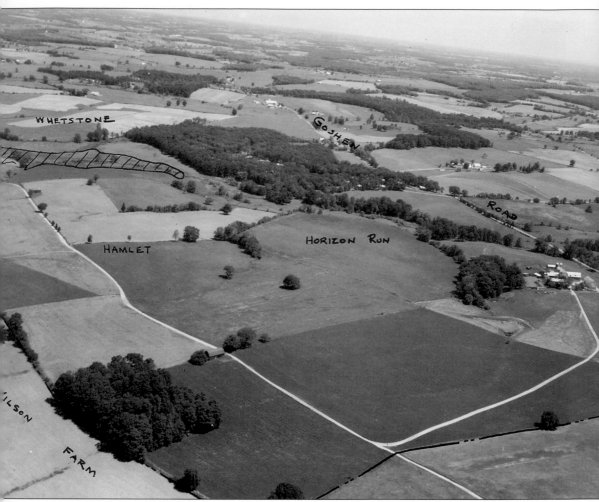

WHETSTONE

GOSHEN

ROAD

HAMLET

HORIZON RUN

ILSON FARM

ENVISIONING A CORRIDOR CITY. As Kettler Brothers Inc. was acquiring land and planning for the new community, the Montgomery County Planning Board was seeking a way to develop a series of corridor cities in the region. The county's 1962 Wedges and Corridors Plan conceived of transportation arteries (corridors) leading out of Washington, DC, with cities separated by green open space (wedges). In 1963, Kettler Brothers Inc. worked closely with the Maryland–National Capital Park and Planning Commission to work out the details of Montgomery Village as a model for the larger plan. The county council approved the ordinance for Montgomery Village in May 1964, and the plans for Montgomery Village were unveiled in November 1964.

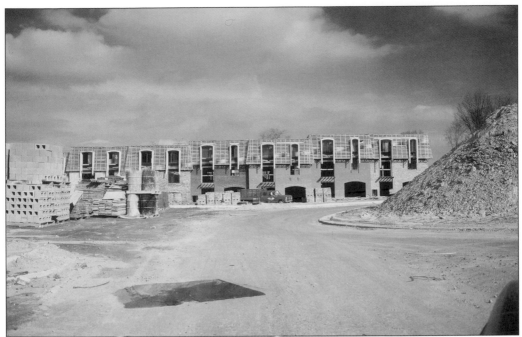

CONSTRUCTION OF THE NEW TOWN BEGINS. After getting approval of the project and the zoning changes in August 1965, construction began in early 1966. The Kettler brothers visited other "new towns" already under construction and worked with experts in land use, design, and marketing. With a single, family-owned firm planning, developing, and building the entire community, Montgomery Village differed from larger new towns like Columbia, Maryland. The Clusters of Stedwick (above) features townhouses, each having its own front and backyard. Sales of these mansard-roofed townhouses began at $31,000. Dick and Eileen Bartik were the first homeowners to go to settlement for their new residence in Montgomery Village (below).

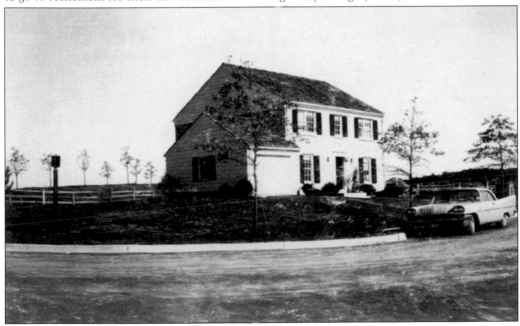

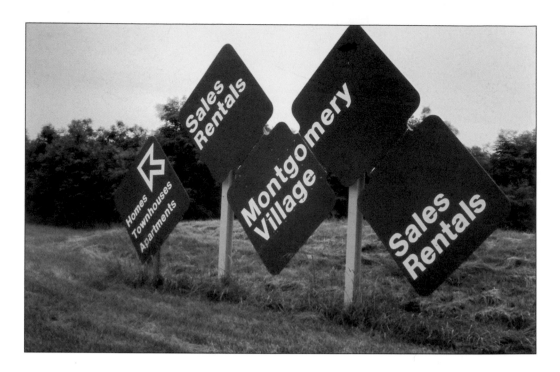

DIVERSITY OF HOUSING OPTIONS. Few communities built at the time offered as diverse a group of housing options as Montgomery Village. Kettler Brothers Inc. developed and built a mixture of garden and high-rise apartments, sale and rental townhouses, and contemporary and detached homes. (Lynda Switzer.)

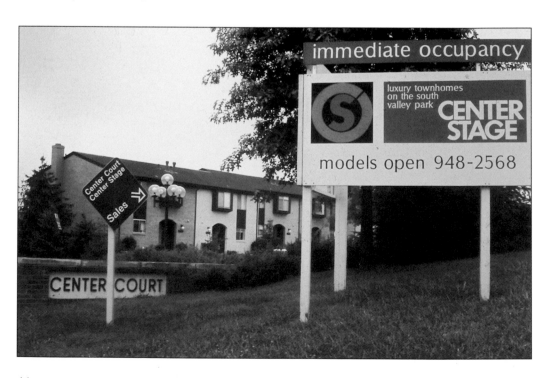

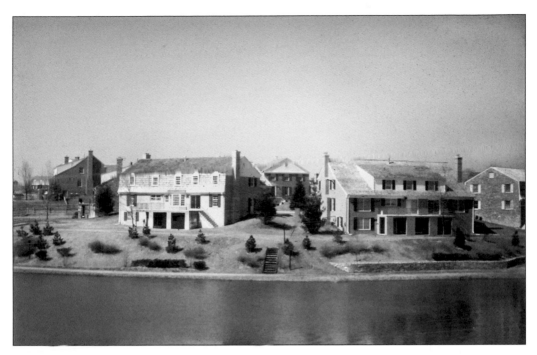

DISTINCTIVE STYLES AND NAMES. Lakeside in the Whetstone neighborhood offered large traditional homes on the shores of Lake Whetstone. A news article from 1971 shows that these four- and five-bedroom houses were priced from $55,000. In Goshenside of Whetstone and the Ridges of Stedwick, medium-sized traditional homes were priced from the upper $30,000s. (Above, Lynda Switzer; below, Peggy Kluge.)

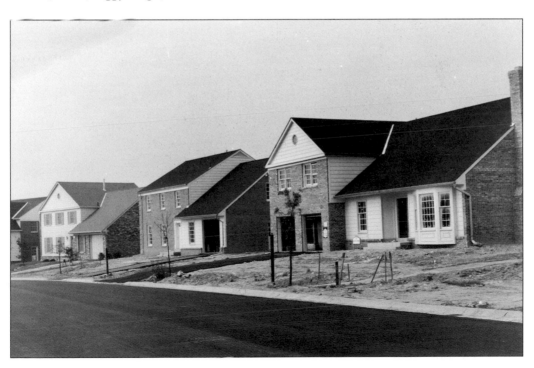

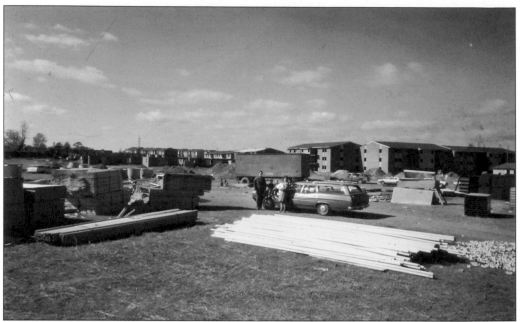

AFFORDABLE HOUSING OPTIONS. Rental units were offered at Mills Choice and Walkers Choice in one-, two-, and three-bedroom models starting at $185 a month in 1971. (Lynda Switzer.)

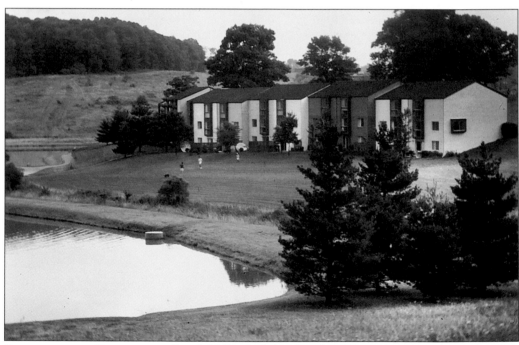

SURROUNDED BY RECREATION. South Valley Park borders three communities with ponds, trees, the Lawn Theater, and playing fields designed to be enjoyed by all residents. The cost of these amenities was taken into consideration by Kettler Brothers Inc. in its budget process so that the entire system could be turned over free and clear to the community organization that would operate the facilities. (Lynda Switzer.)

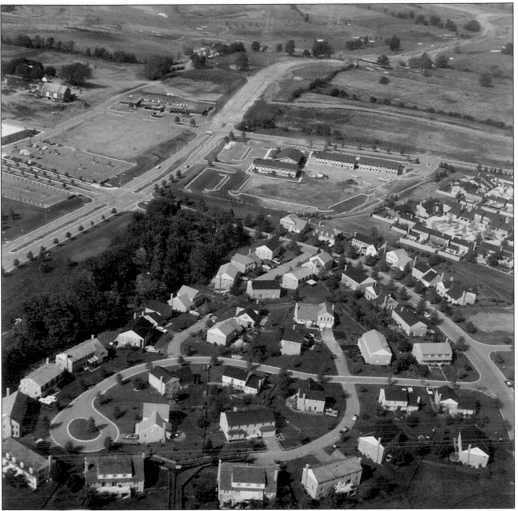

EMPHASIS ON OPEN SPACE. The Kettler brothers had a creative vision to build their new community surrounded by open space, setting aside 557 acres for that purpose. Homes were arranged in clusters to facilitate a local identity, including swimming pools, community centers, parks, and public schools for each neighborhood. The community as a whole shared a 135-acre golf course, police station, firehouse, and library site. To create these communities, Kettler Brothers Inc. constructed 7.5 miles of major arterial roads and installed lighting along the highways and residential streets. Utilities were buried underground. Thirty miles of streets, as well as community centers, pools, and parks, were to be maintained privately. These facilities were part of a growing practice of builders and developers providing many of the services that the local county government and taxpayers had in the past underwritten.

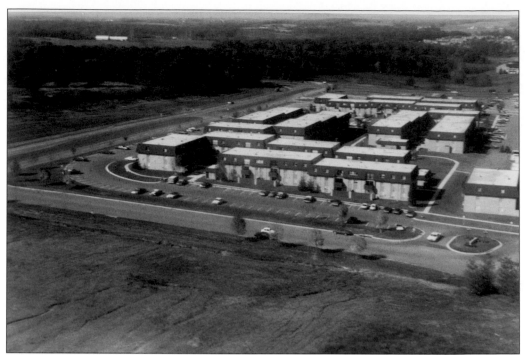

UNIQUE DESIGN. Montgomery Village was unique from a design point of view. Kettler Brothers Inc. experimented with many different housing styles and neighborhood layouts. A broad range of housing types and costs accommodated the individual lifestyles and incomes of the residents. Each neighborhood had a distinct style but also blended in with the rest of the community due to the careful planning and the use of similar materials. The Hamlet Apartments (above, today known as Cider Mill) were intended to appeal to younger residents who worked in the area. Traditional single-family homes in Lakeside (below) and Goshenside of Whetstone were marketed to families. (Above, MVF; below, Peggy Kluge.)

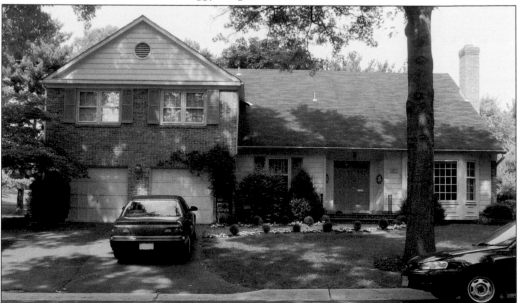

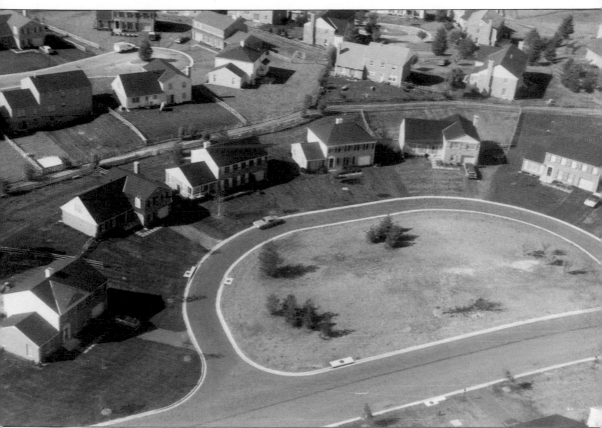

CREATING A VILLAGE FEEL. The "new town" concept of cluster development harkened back to New England villages, where houses sat on a common green with common pastureland to the rear. In the new community, homes were built on relatively small lots closer to the street with large amounts of green space dedicated to communal use. The open space to the rear of the homes was utilized to create paths, play areas, green spaces, and separation between each home. Oxcart Place in Goshenside of Whetstone featured a large common area where children would play.

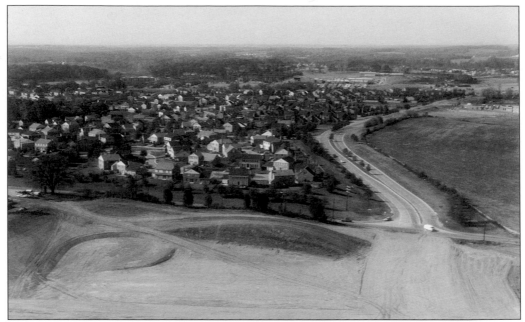

PRESERVING THE NATURAL ENVIRONMENT. The streets were designed to create a sense of community and also to preserve the natural environment. Streets were not arranged in the typical suburban grid pattern. Neighborhoods were designed along winding roads that sought to preserve the natural contours of the farmland, with its open spaces and rolling hills. Houses were laid out in courts or circular patterns to bring neighbors together and create a sense of community. Neighborhood layouts included private streets, culs-de-sac, open spaces, and walkable paths that connected the community and created an appealing atmosphere.

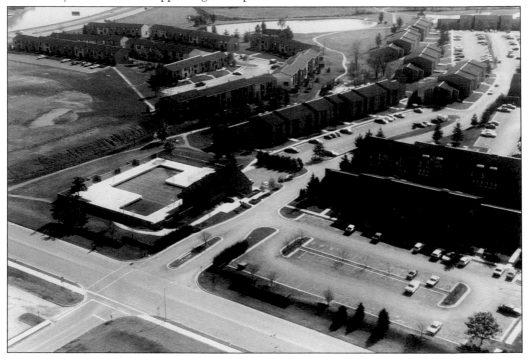

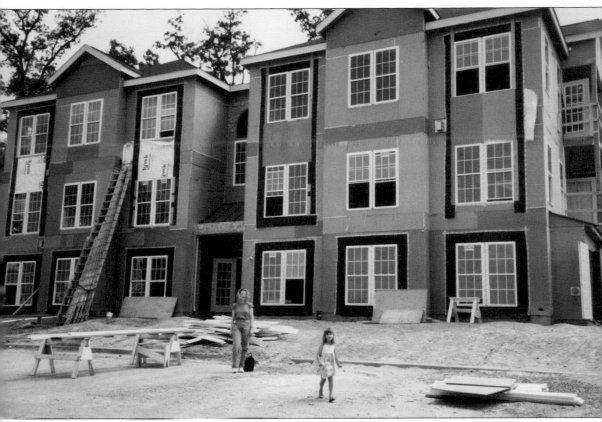

THE NEED FOR AFFORDABLE HOUSING. As the price of land in Montgomery County began to increase rapidly, builders in the area had to come up with innovative land-use ideas. In 1976, Clarence Kettler reflected that he believed all citizens are entitled to an affordable house, and he felt this could be achieved in an ecologically sound way by building high-density housing. These new kinds of homes would be "carefully done and interesting structures with a good environment, good privacy, and low maintenance. The yard might be on the roof instead of outside their door, and it might be a wood deck instead of a lawn." One example of this new dense housing was Park Place II, shown here in 1979. (Diane Coleman.)

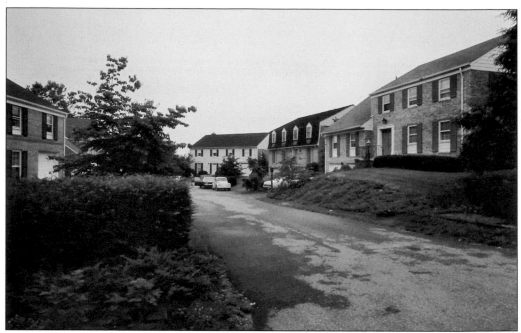

Balancing Environmental Stewardship with Economic Benefits. In the 1960s, Kettler Brothers Inc. used innovative techniques in storm water management in building its new town. Today, developers still advocate the use of these techniques to reduce water pollution. For example, smaller street widths with fewer impervious surfaces reduced building costs and eased storm water runoff. The results were increased green space and a lessened environmental impact (above, in Whetstone). Swales beside the streets slowed storm water runoff and provided for the absorption of the water (below, in The Points). (Lynda Switzer.)

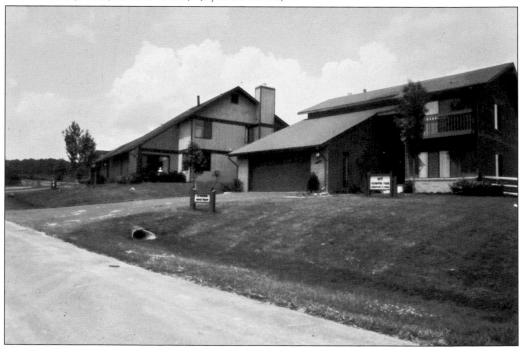

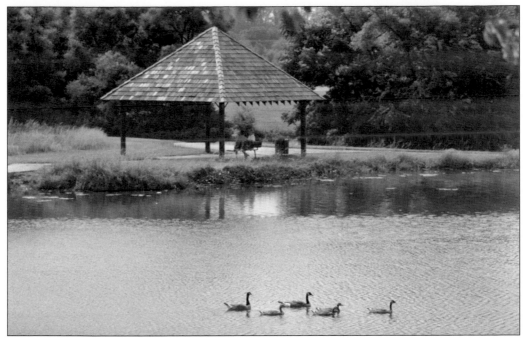

BUILDING FOR A NEW ENVIRONMENT. The storm water management system for Montgomery Village was environmentally, aesthetically, and recreationally integrated. When buildings, streets, driveways, and parking lots were constructed in the area, they increased the amount of runoff and pollution from rain. The lakes and ponds slowed down the drainage of storm water and allowed many impurities to settle out and reduce the burden downstream. Lake Whetstone actually provided storm water management for some of Montgomery Village and much of Gaithersburg. North Creek Lake provides storm water management for other parts of the Village. In addition, the lakes and ponds were made into aesthetic, recreational areas that formed important amenities for the new town, including the gazebos shown above. There are 12 gazebos with the same distinctive style in the open spaces in Montgomery Village. (Above, Jane Wilder; below, MVF.)

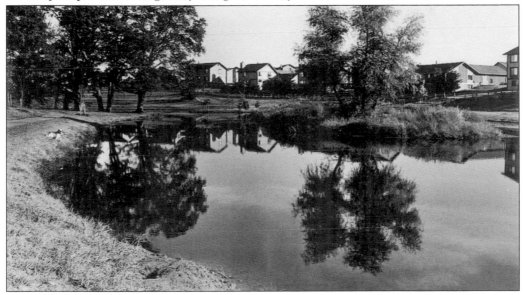

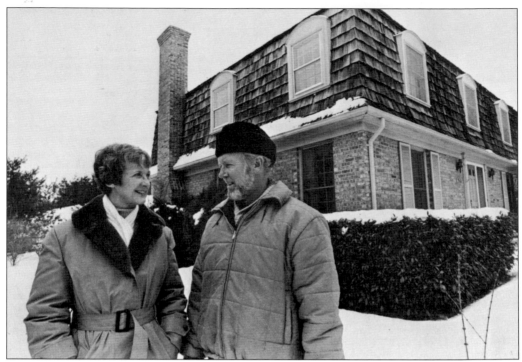

FIRST RESIDENTS MOVE TO LAKESIDE OF WHETSTONE. By the time Jim and Ruth Crosby, seen above, moved into their new home in 1967, Kettler Brothers Inc. had spent $11 million to develop the new community. By 1971, more than 1,000 families, including the women pictured below, lived in Montgomery Village in distinctive communities of different housing styles and prices. (Below, Jerrold Ward.)

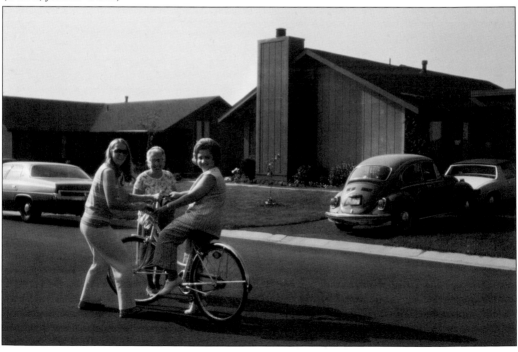

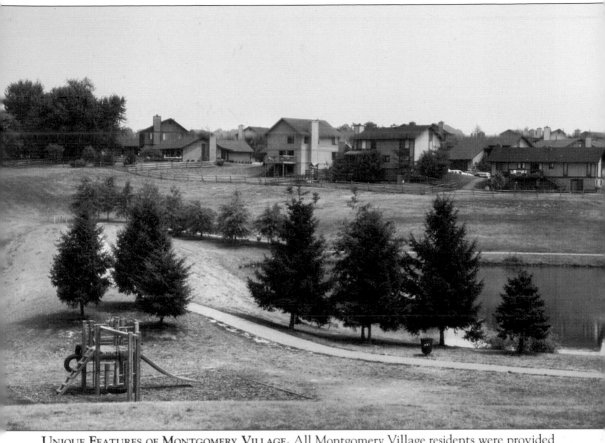

UNIQUE FEATURES OF MONTGOMERY VILLAGE. All Montgomery Village residents were provided with a system of open spaces and recreational facilities located throughout the Village. The MVF was established in 1966 to maintain and operate the common property in the community. Bike paths, ball fields, swimming pools, community centers, parks, a nature center, the Lawn Theater, lakes, and ponds were the many facilities available for common use. The foundation also provided architectural control to maintain the visual harmony of the communities. (Roslyn Price.)

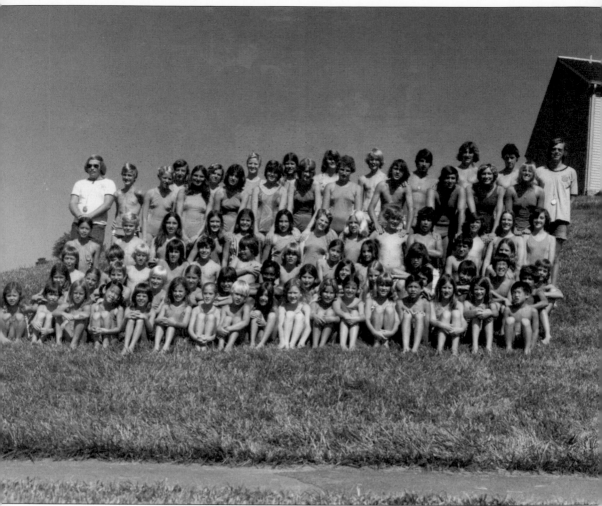

EMPHASIS ON FAMILIES. Montgomery Village was intended from the beginning to be a community for families raising children. Most recreational facilities were available to residents by virtue of their automatic membership in the MVF. Residents paid a separate assessment fee to cover the cost of these facilities. The Montgomery Village Health and Swim Center (later the YMCA) and the golf club were available to residents for a membership fee. Together, these private and public amenities were a great asset and provided a level of recreation services beyond what other residents in Montgomery County had access to in the 1970s. There was strong participation and sense of pride on the Montgomery Village swim teams that were organized around the community pools. In the winter, many teams continued to swim at the indoor pool. In 1973, the Stedwick Sharks gather on the hill behind the pool for a team photograph. (Mathew Lutz.)

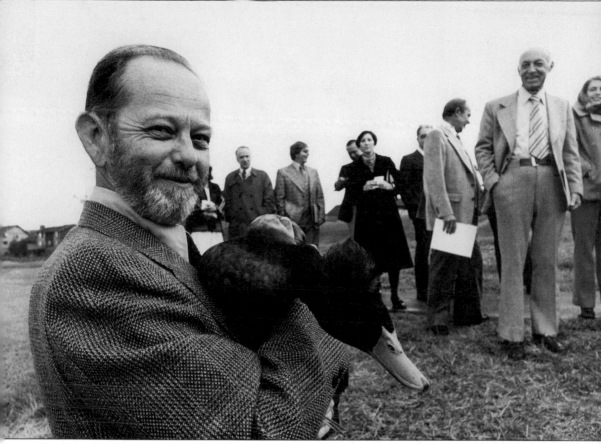

THE FIRST PRESIDENT OF THE HOMES CORPORATION, WILLIAM N. HURLEY JR. Each purchaser of a home in Montgomery Village, whether a single-family house or a condominium, automatically became a member of both a local homes corporation or condominium association and the MVF. In Montgomery Village, the homeowners association was known as the Homes Corporation. Kettler Brothers Inc. wanted to identify that the homeowners group was different from voluntary citizens' associations. As in other "new towns," the homes corporations provided a level of community service beyond what the county could provide. The composition of the corporation evolved over time to a representative government. William "Bill" Hurley Jr. served as the first president of each of the homeowners' corporations in the early years, until residents could elect representatives. This dedicated man was directly responsible for the relationship between Kettler Brothers Inc. and the residents of Montgomery Village. This photograph was taken at the dedication of North Creek Lake in 1977. (William N. Hurley III.)

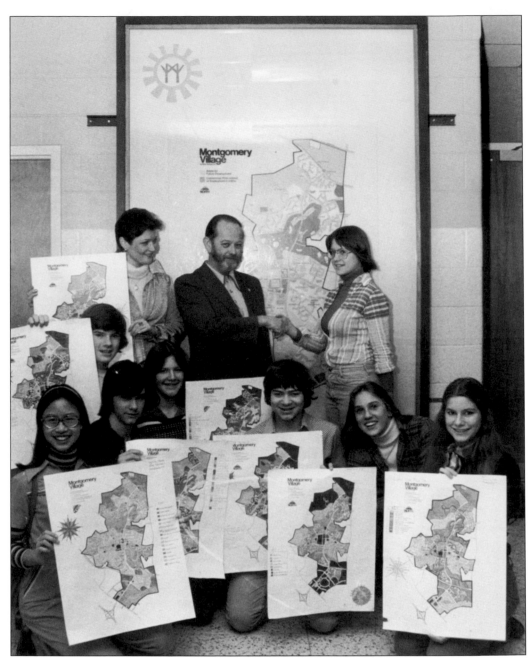

MR. MONTGOMERY VILLAGE. Bill Hurley was an officer of Kettler Brothers Inc. for over 20 years. From the beginning of the project in 1965, he was named coordinator of the Montgomery Village Project and had responsibility for governmental relationships, zoning, long-range planning, legislative liaison, and other matters related to the planning and review process. In 1987, he published *Montgomery Village: A New Town*. Written at the time of the Village's 20th anniversary, this book shares some of the early background of the Village's development, the history of the area, and the previous owners of the land. Hurley writes about the people who had a vision for what this "new town" could be and looked toward the future. In this photograph, Hurley is shown with students from Montgomery Village Junior High School around 1977. (William N. Hurley III.)

Four

NATURAL LANDMARKS

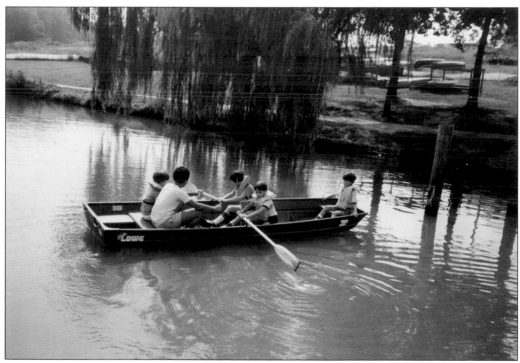

MONTGOMERY VILLAGE BOASTS 12 PARKS, INCLUDING FOUR LAKES. Most parks and lakes are connected by bike paths and are easily accessible from anywhere in Montgomery Village. The parks offer ample opportunity for enjoyment of all kinds. Whenever possible, Kettler Brothers Inc. worked hard to preserve the natural beauty of the land. Lake Whetstone, seen here, was built in 1967 and covers approximately 27 acres.

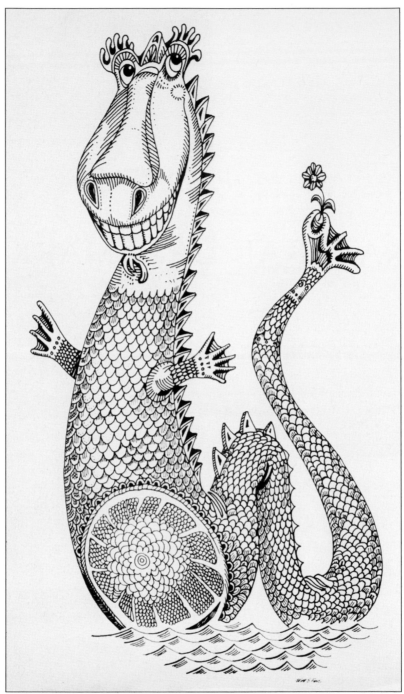

THE LEGEND OF LAKE WHETSTONE. According to legend, this friendly dragon moved in shortly after Kettler Brothers Inc. finished building the lake and has happily inhabited the waters ever since. The legend and original cartoon rendering of this Village denizen, formerly published in Kettler Brothers Inc. sales materials, is reprinted periodically in the Kids' Pages of the *Montgomery Village News* to keep it alive in the imaginations of current residents. (Drawing by William S. Farr.)

OPPORTUNITIES TO ENJOY THE LAND. From miles of paths to lakes of various sizes, the Village offers options for exercise and enjoyment to residents of all ages. The Village features ball fields, playgrounds, boating and fishing on Lake Whetstone and other lakes, and plenty of scenery for pure enjoyment. From the beginning, there has been a great effort to balance enjoyment of the parks and green spaces with protection of the Village's natural resources. (Above, MVF; below, Howard Clark.)

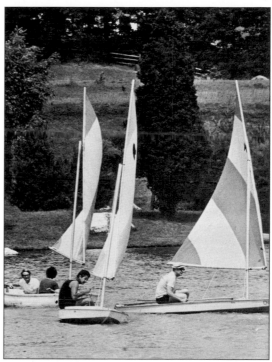

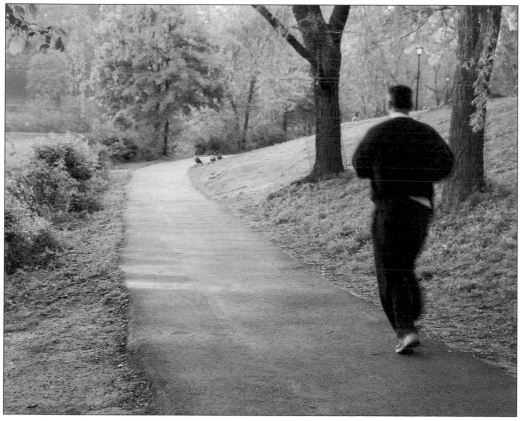

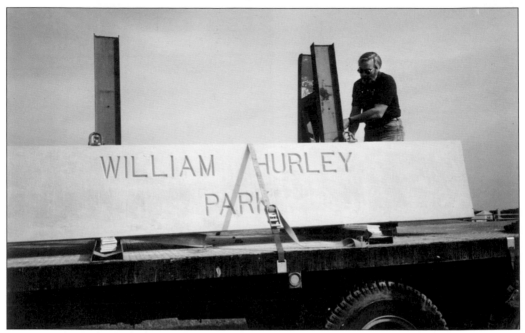

WILLIAM HURLEY PARK, 1986. Bill Hurley was instrumental in Montgomery Village's beginnings. He worked for Kettler Brothers Inc. and served on the board of the MVF, looking out for his fellow citizens for many years. He was the first president of each of the Village boards, mentoring them until the residents were able to take over. William Hurley Park was dedicated in his name when he retired in 1986. The park sits on nine acres at the north end of Montgomery Village and features a swimming pool, ball fields, picnic areas, playgrounds, and basketball courts. Hurley passed away in 2003.

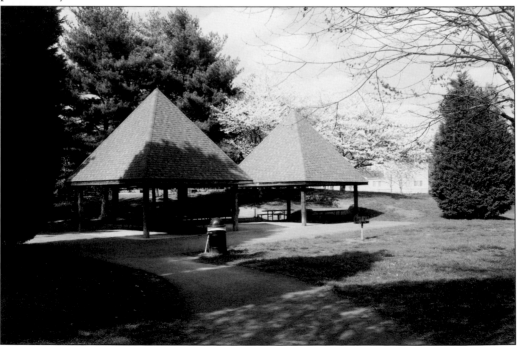

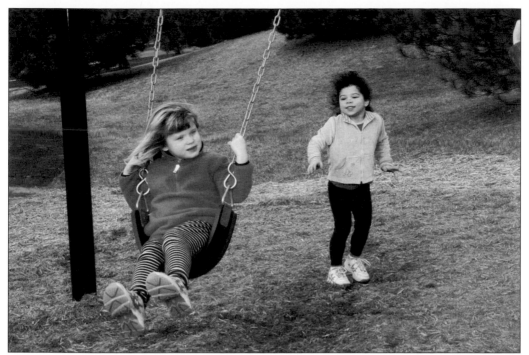

MARTIN P. ROY PARK. Martin Roy Park sits on the east side of the Village and includes a play area, baseball field, and stone sitting area. Besides ample opportunities for athletes to enjoy the natural spaces in the Village, most parks include playgrounds for children. The Village's green spaces are meant to be enjoyed by people of all ages.

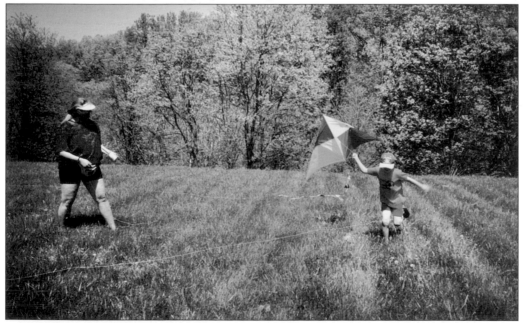

FLYING KITES AT APPLE RIDGE RECREATION AREA. Clarence Kettler said, "I love anything to do with the water. And I love children. And I love nature and flowers and growing things." All of these elements can be seen in some form in each of Montgomery Village's parks.

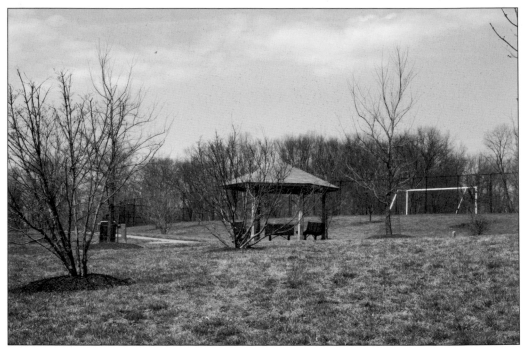

MILTON M. KAUFMANN PARK. Milton Kaufmann is a longtime resident of Montgomery Village dedicated to environmental issues and promoting conservation. This park includes athletic fields, paths, a pond, and playgrounds. Construction of the park was a joint venture of the MVF and Montgomery County. The park was dedicated on May 6, 2006.

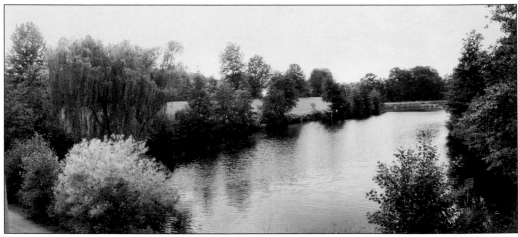

LAKE MARION PARK. Lake Marion is located at the northern end of Montgomery Village in East Village, adjacent to the newest of four community centers. The lake is 3.1 acres, and the park includes a gazebo, paths, grills, and picnic areas.

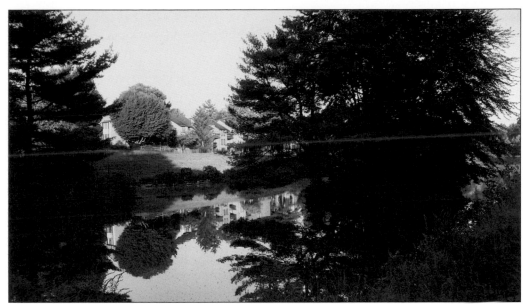

NORTH CREEK LAKE. North Creek Lake Park is the largest park in the Village at 83.7 acres. The lake covers 6.5 acres and is surrounded by paved paths. At one end of the lake is the North Creek Stream Valley. The park also features two playgrounds and picnic areas. (Roslyn Price.)

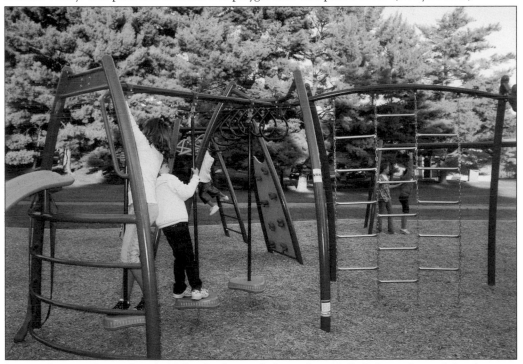

SOUTH VALLEY PARK. South Valley Park was dedicated in 1968. It has a larger lake that was divided into three smaller lakes when the Village Mall was built. The lake naturally flooded 11 acres. The lakes and streams were intended to act as a storm water management system. Today, South Valley Park is home to the Lawn Theater, ball fields, playgrounds, picnic areas, paths, and plenty of open green space.

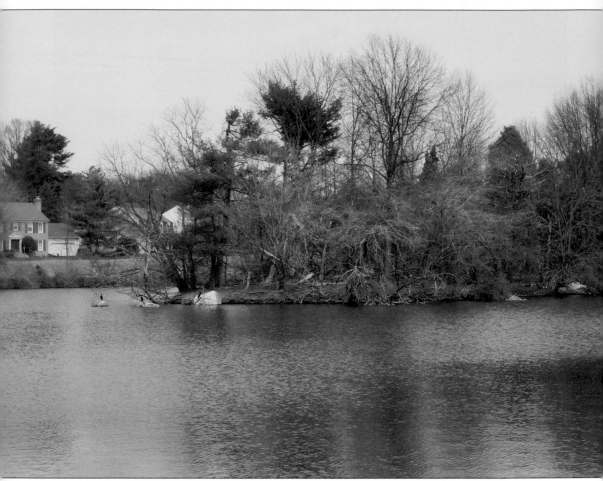

AN ISLAND FOR WILDLIFE. Early on, Lake Whetstone Island was a popular place for sunbathing. Until 1981, the island served as the launching site for Fourth of July fireworks. In the years since, the island has been off-limits to people, and a variety of wildlife now flourishes there. (Roslyn Price.)

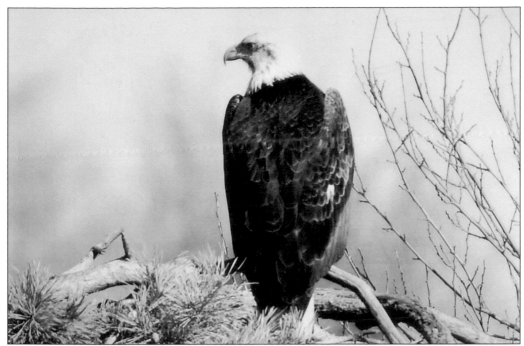

NATIVE BIRDS. When human access to Lake Whetstone Island was restricted, it became home to a myriad of birds, many of which are native species to the area. Among the species that can be found in Montgomery Village are great blue herons, egrets, cormorants, and the occasional visiting eagle. The Village was even home to a single mute swan for several years. Canada geese are also common in the Village. It is not unusual to be stuck behind cars that have stopped to allow a gaggle of geese and goslings to cross the road. (Above, Ski Aller; below, MVF.)

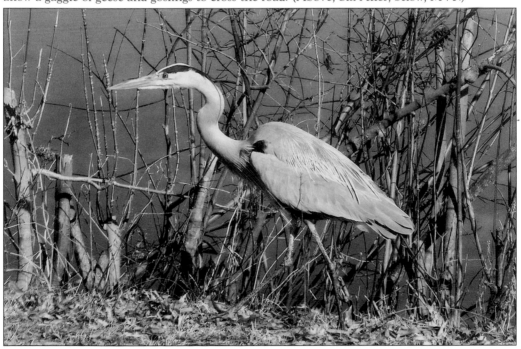

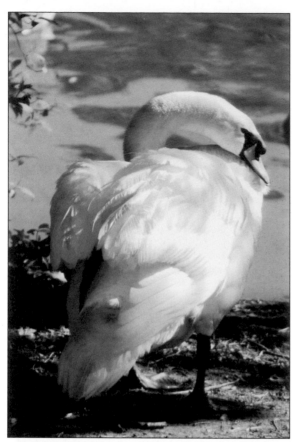

MUTE SWAN. For a time, Lake Whetstone was home to a single mute swan, which became a beloved sight to Villagers. Following the swan's passing, a memorial was planted at the lakeside in its honor (below). (Left, Ski Aller; below, MVF.)

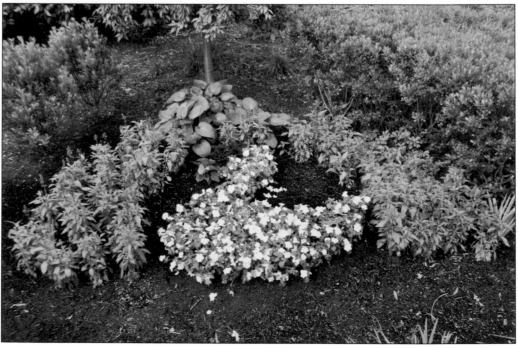

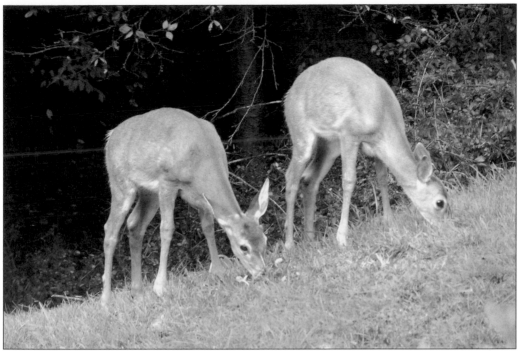

OTHER VILLAGE WILDLIFE. Although Montgomery Village is a suburban environment, there is plenty of wildlife to be found besides the many bird species. Many of the lakes are stocked with fish. When Lake Walker (today the site of Lakeforest Mall) was first constructed, there were freshwater clams present. Deer, rabbits, and groundhogs are abundant in the area, and the occasional fox can be seen. Even as Montgomery Village has grown and changed, a great effort has been made to preserve the green spaces and to respect the wildlife that inhabits the area. (Above, Diane Levy; below, Ski Aller.)

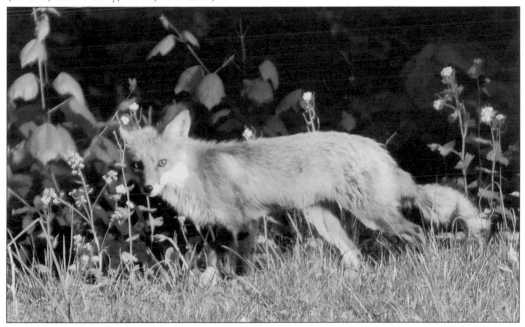

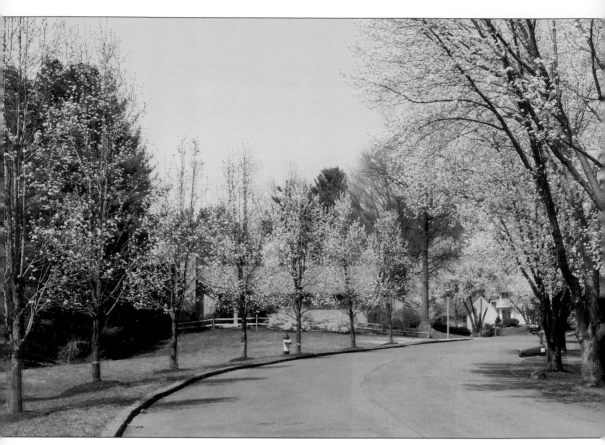

MONTGOMERY VILLAGE, TREE CITY. Montgomery Village is a Tree City, a title that has been earned for the past 22 years. In 1966, about 10,000 pin oaks were brought in from Laurel, Maryland, to be planted along the roads in the new community. Azaleas were brought in from Rockville, Maryland, and at various times, tree farms were planted in the Village to grow white pines for planting in new neighborhoods.

Five

PLACES

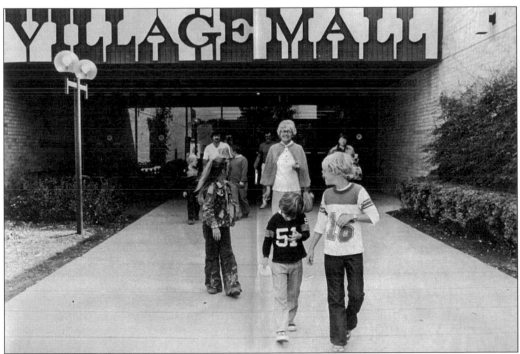

VILLAGE MALL ENTRANCE, 1977. The Village Mall opened an all-season indoor shopping center on Montgomery Village Avenue in 1970. Known fondly by residents as "the small mall with it all," it not only provided convenient shopping to Village residents but was also the venue for many special events, including concerts, antique shows, art shows, and dances. Kettler Brothers Inc. corporate headquarters was also located in the Village Mall.

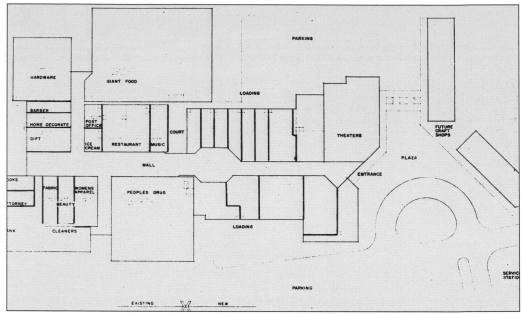

MAP OF MALL INTERIOR. Taken from the *Living Magazine* 1975 issue, the original diagram of the Village Mall shows existing and proposed shops. When opened, the mall contained 18 convenience shops, including a drugstore, grocery, bank, hardware, post office, dress shop, shoe store, and Greek restaurant.

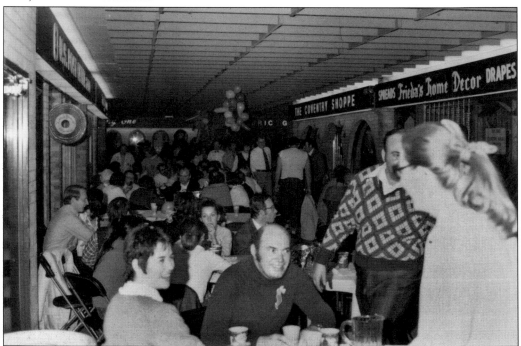

MALL INTERIOR VIEWS. This corridor shows a large holiday party held in the mall, which was a gathering place for friends and family. The Village Mall Merchants Association hosted many special events, often in partnership with other Village groups such as the Women's Club or the MVF. (Peggy Kluge.)

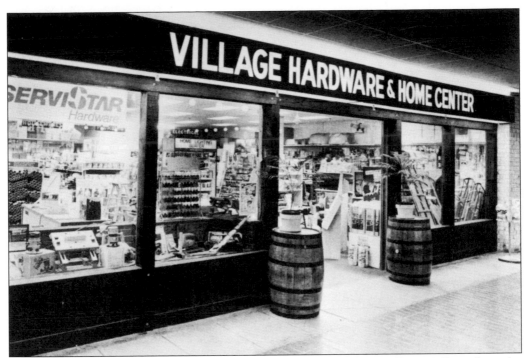

VILLAGE HARDWARE. The Village Hardware and Home Center in the Village Mall was from the start popular for its friendly hometown service as much as its convenience, where one could find not only the tools one needed but also advice on how to use them. In early years, the store was owned by Kettler Brothers Inc. and managed by George Aubin, who had worked for the developer and designed many of the Village facilities. (Sherry Witt.)

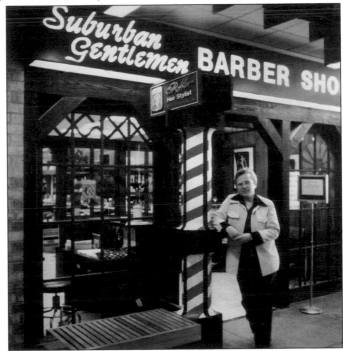

BARBER SHOP. The Suburban Gentlemen Barber/Hair Designers shop was the site of many a Village child's first haircut. Owner Bill Wilder was an active member of the Village Mall Merchants Association, which sponsored many of the mall's special events.

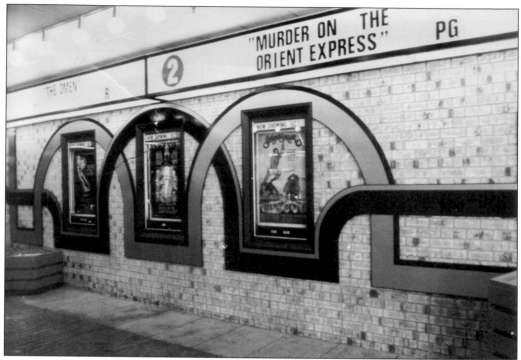

MOVIE THEATER. The ceramic tile wall design shows the Village Mall Cinemas 3 movie theater entrance. The theater launched in September 1975, when an addition to the original Montgomery Village Mall opened with 16 shops. The adjacent Village Quarter opened in 1976 with shops and offices and additional office space or residential quarters occupying the second story.

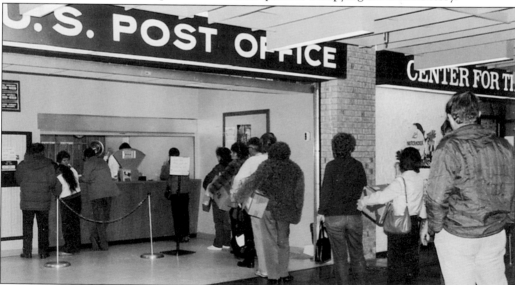

US POST OFFICE INSIDE THE VILLAGE MALL. This view of the US post office was taken from near the mall's entrance with people waiting in line. Following the renovation of the mall in 1990, the post office relocated to a freestanding building nearby at the corner of Stedwick and Watkins Mill Roads, and it now offers the public drive-through drop-off mail service in addition to full-service post office functions.

THE NEW VILLAGE CENTER. The new Montgomery Village Center sign was dedicated in the early 1990s. Here, then MVF board members Linc Perley (left) and Frank Mondell (far right) participate in the dedication with representatives from Washington Real Estate Investment Trust, which purchased the center in 1992.

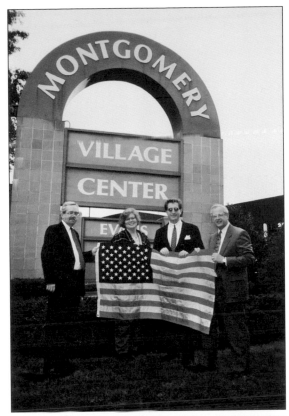

RENOVATED EXTERIOR AT THE VILLAGE CENTER. This exterior view of the Village Center depicts the finished renovation, showing the open-air half-circular pass-through entry sidewalk (now a driveway) and the Village Café sign visible through the young tree.

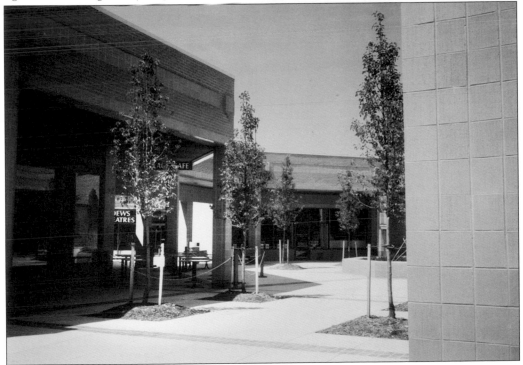

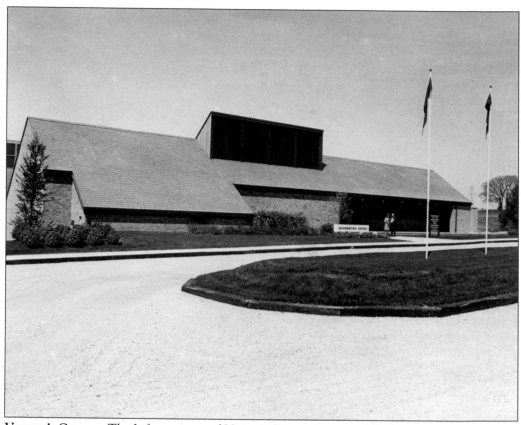

VISITOR'S CENTER. The Information and Visitor's Center showcased the home corporations' and condominium associations' homes and condominiums for sale and featured all amenities available in the Village. The center closed once most of the new properties had been sold.

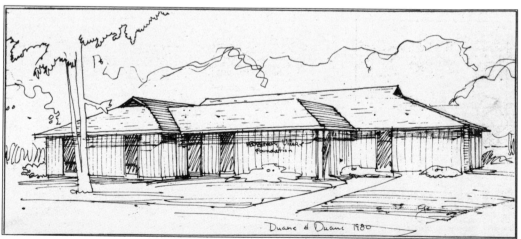

MONTGOMERY VILLAGE FOUNDATION OFFICE. The MVF offices were first located in the Professional Center and then moved to North Creek Community Center after it opened in July 1975. In the early 1980s, a site that had been held for a potential elementary school on Apple Ridge Road was turned over to the foundation, and the current offices were built, along with an adjacent maintenance facility.

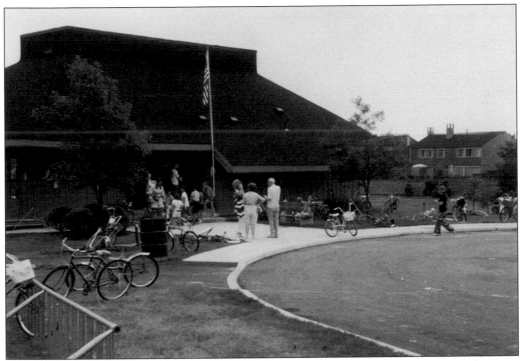

WHETSTONE COMMUNITY CENTER, 1970. Opening in August 1968 with a 25-meter pool, tennis courts, a community building, and a tot lot, Whetstone was the first of four community centers located through the Village. It was the venue for many of the early foundation programs and special events, including the annual Fourth of July Celebration.

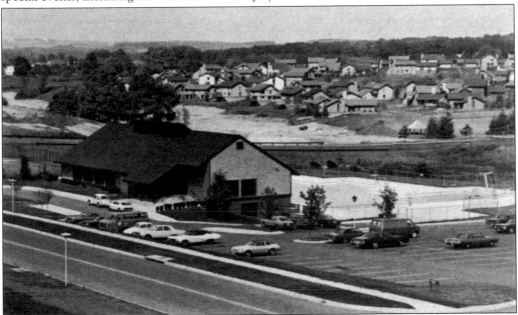

NORTH CREEK COMMUNITY CENTER. This overview shows the North Creek Community Center, which opened in July 1975, featuring a 50-meter Olympic-size pool. Other features at the center include meeting and classrooms, lighted tennis courts, and a playground.

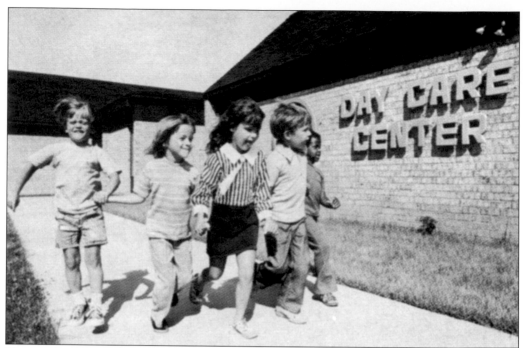

Montgomery Village Day Care Center. The day care center is located at the corner of Montgomery Village Avenue and Lost Knife Road, just past the official entrance to the Village after leaving the city of Gaithersburg.

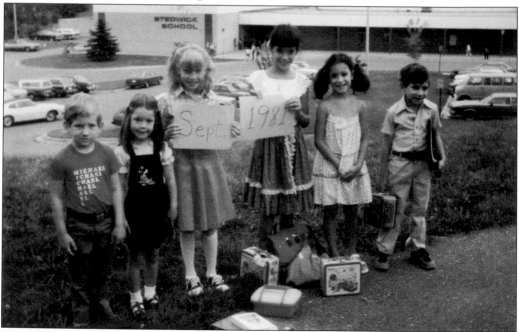

Kindergarteners' First Day at Stedwick Elementary School. Stedwick opened in January 1975 as one of the seven elementary schools serving Montgomery Village. The school was designed with non-traditional—and somewhat controversial—"open" classrooms, with combined grade levels to enable students to better learn at their own pace. (Joan Ferrante.)

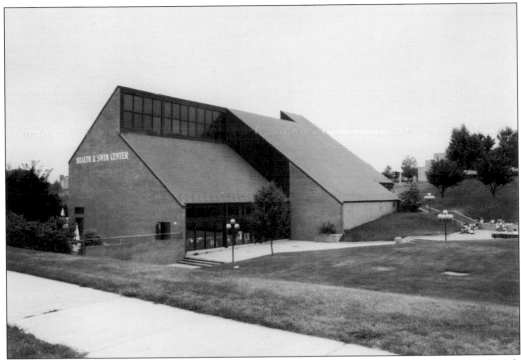

MONTGOMERY VILLAGE SWIM CENTER. The swim center opened for membership in 1968 with year-round swimming, sauna, exercise room, and paddle tennis. Later, the facility was donated by Kettler Brothers Inc. to the YMCA. It remained a popular hub for indoor exercise and swimming until March 2007, when it closed its doors and was torn down to make way for a new strip shopping area.

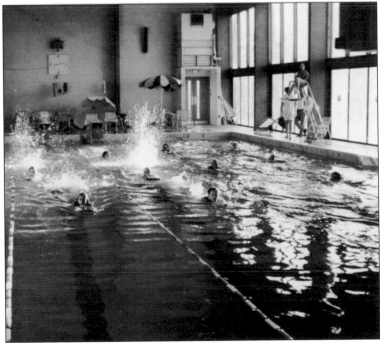

YMCA INDOOR POOL. The indoor pool of the YMCA continued to attract large numbers of recreational swimmers and provide practice space for off-season swim teams. Many a Village resident began his day with a predawn lap swim before commuting to his job.

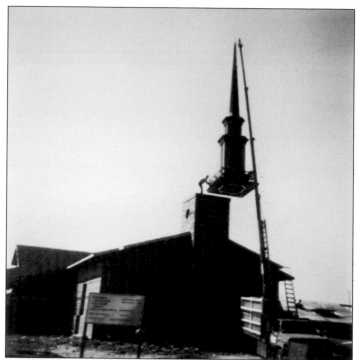

PLACES OF WORSHIP. The original Land Use Plan, adopted in 1965, indicated eight possible sites for church uses. The National Council of Churches originally wished to be involved in the assignment of church locations, but eventually it was left to the individual denomination to contact the developer. In October 1977, construction began on the temple of the Church of Jesus Christ of Latter-day Saints. Villagers now enjoy numerous religious opportunities, including Mormon, Jewish, Methodist, Lutheran, Baptist, Catholic, and others. (Jim Childers.)

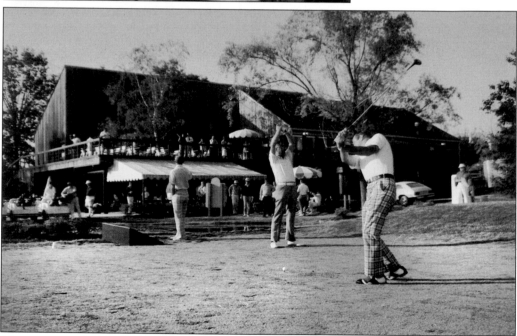

MONTGOMERY VILLAGE GOLF CLUB. The Montgomery Village Golf Course, comprising 150 acres, was completed in September 1967, in time for the 1968 season. The clubhouse, pictured here and known later as the Willow Tree Inn, hosted many special events, including the annual Harden and Weaver Tournament, which raised substantial funds for Children's Hospital. Upstairs provided elegant dining, while downstairs, the Grill Room fed and watered tired golfers finishing a round on the course.

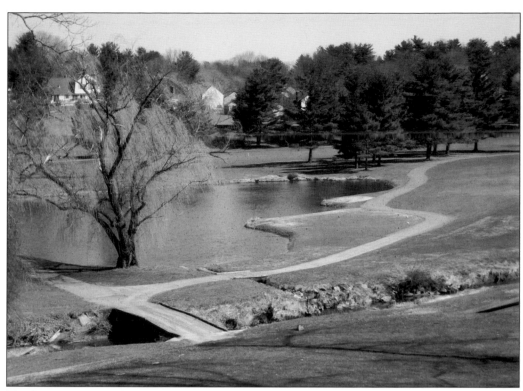

THE LEGEND OF THE ELEVENTH HOLE. A "glubb" is rumored to be a very shy creature, able to disguise itself as a small, stationary shrub and is thought to frequent the fairways of championship golf courses, feeding on golf balls. Though no one in the Village has claimed to have actually seen a glubb, evidence of its existence has been noted by certain individuals of irreproachable character who regularly play golf on the par-72 golf course. According to their testimony, the alleged glubb is partial to the 11th fairway, where frequently, after hitting a perfect drive straight down the center of the fairway, one can arrive at where the ball should surely be and not find it, even after looking under every nearby bush and shrub. What happened to it? That pesky glubb must have snatched it up! (Above, Roslyn Price; right, drawing by William S. Farr.)

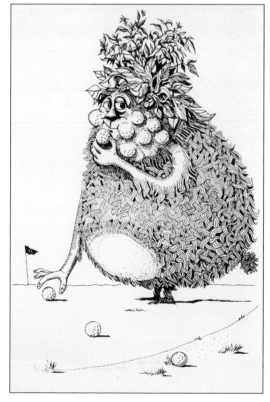

81

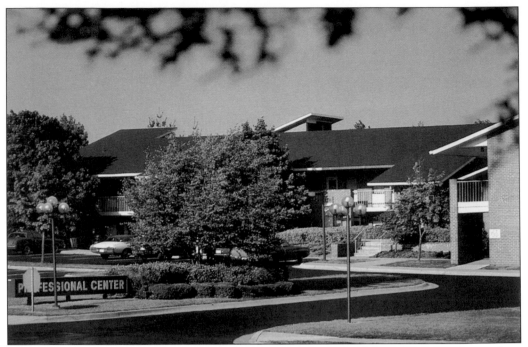

PROFESSIONAL CENTER. This panoramic overview of the Professional Center entrance is seen from Montgomery Village Avenue across from the mall before the sign was changed. The first of seven buildings around a courtyard opened in January 1971 featuring a variety of medical offices and other professional services, with a freestanding pharmacy facing Montgomery Village Avenue.

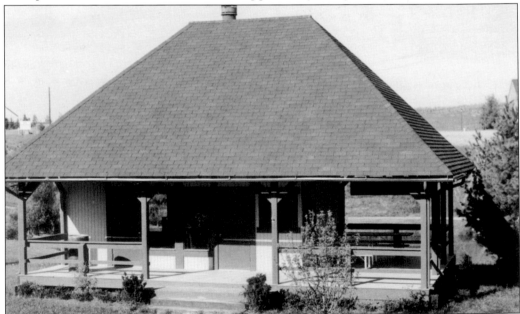

NORTH CREEK NATURE CENTER, 1978. The nature center was dedicated in October 1977 as part of the North Creek Lake Park. The nature center can be seen from Montgomery Village Avenue and accessed by paths from The Points and the lake. Many Scout groups and nature workshops have met in the rustic little center, often for a special exhibit or lesson.

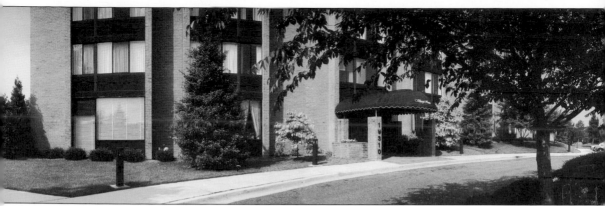

Village House Entrance, 1978. This view was taken from the original cover of the four-page color foldout brochure when Village House opened in 1978. It featured independent and assisted living residences, offering one- or two-bedroom rental apartments to people over 50 years old. The Sunrise management team offered concierge services when it took over operations in 1993. CNL Investors purchased the property and the business in 2011 with the idea of renovating while keeping the Sunrise team to maintain the residents' quality of life. The elegant interior decor enhanced the amenities offered: a library, a country store, card rooms, a large banquet room with dietary options, and a chauffeured minibus to shops and other Village conveniences. (Sunrise.)

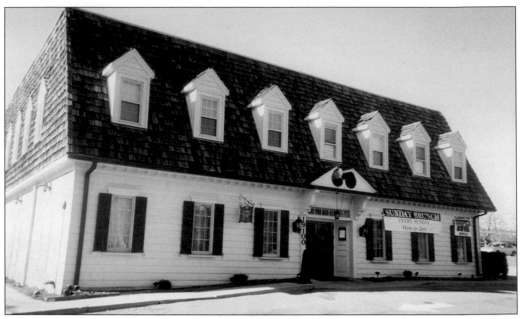

Sir Walter Raleigh Inn. The Colonial-style Sir Walter Raleigh Inn, adjacent to the Village Mall, was where Villagers regularly celebrated a nice dinner out or a special family event. Perched on a hill looking out on Montgomery Village Avenue, it was a cherished landmark for many years until it closed in 2005. (Jerry Cosker.)

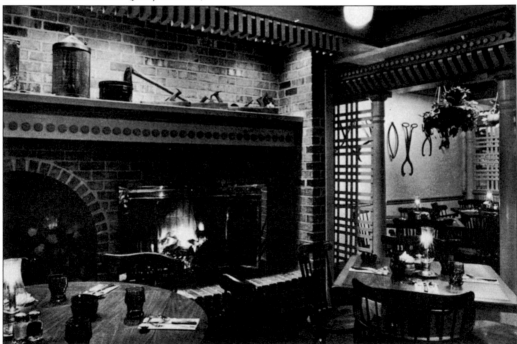

Sir Walter Raleigh Inn Interior. This interior view shows a brick hearth, seating, and charming decor. The four principal owners (Carl Sturges, Tom Bradford, Walter Ward, and Dennis Hopnick), who also owned 16 other restaurants, built this inn at the Montgomery Village Mall in 1980, locating it at the corner of Stedwick Road and Montgomery Village Avenue. (Sherry Witt.)

Six

PEOPLE

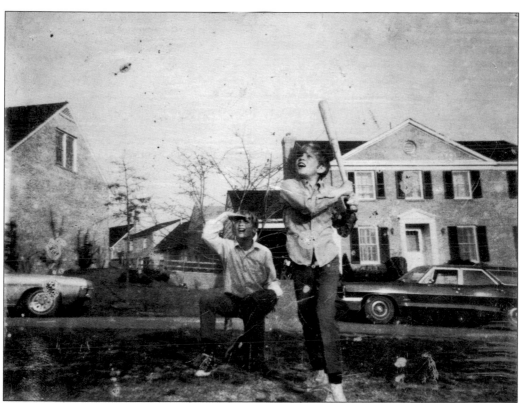

ORGANIZING THE FIRST TEAMS, 1969. Neighbors Don Heck and Jack O'Connell, who had 11 children between them, formed baseball teams to play in the Upper Montgomery County Baseball League. Teams included any children who attended school in Montgomery Village. The teams won their divisions, and the championship game was played at Whetstone Elementary on the Fourth of July. Two years later, Heck and O'Connell founded the Montgomery Village Sports Association. (Marilyn O'Connell.)

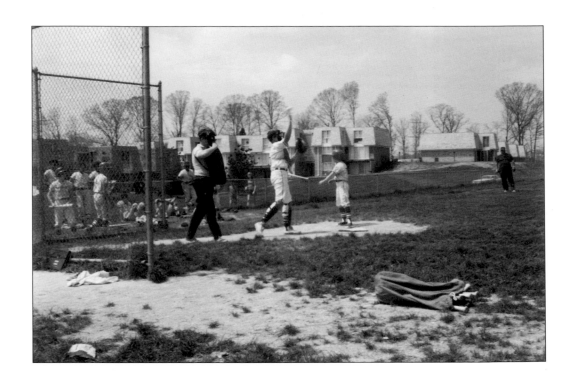

Montgomery Village Sports Association (MVSA). In 1971, the MVSA was founded with 18 baseball teams as well as other sports teams, including football, basketball, and swimming. William Schmitz was the original chairman, Ken Owens coached football, Jack O'Connell coached baseball, and Don Heck was the MVSA president. The encouragement and values of the MVSA, coaches, and community resulted in many athletes who went on to excel in college sports, including Owens's sons, who played college football. Two MVSA players even went on to play professional football. By 1978, there were over 1,000 boys and girls participating in the MVSA.

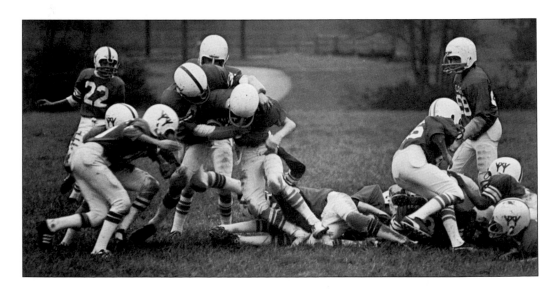

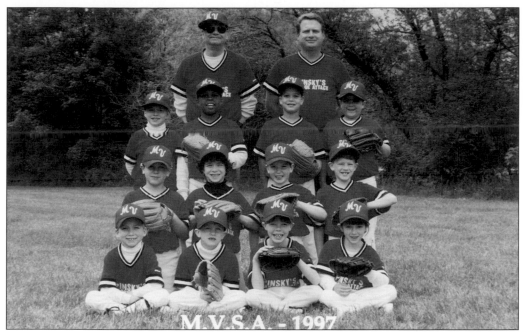

DON HECK AND JACK O'CONNELL. Heck wrote a mission for the organization: "Our goals are to develop athletic skills, encourage good sportsmanship, and foster an appreciation for responsibility, leadership, citizenship, and moral dedication. . . . Success in each program is measured in participation, fun and fundamentals, not solely in won-loss records. . . . The way they play today may very well be the way they'll live tomorrow." O'Connell's dream for the MVSA was realized through coaching generations of children, including his own grandchildren, one of whom is in the first row. Jack is the man wearing sunglasses; his son is beside him. (Marilyn O'Connell.)

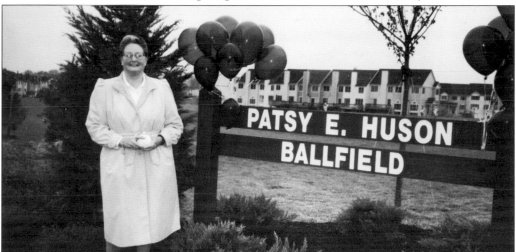

PAT HUSON. Girls' sports in Montgomery Village began with the Husons. When the MVSA denied the Huson girls' request to join teams, Pat Huson found gym time for girls' sports activities and became the girls' basketball commissioner. In 1971, she organized girls' softball, struggling to find coaches and fields. Nevertheless, the girls' sports program quickly became competitive. In 1992, the Patsy E. Huson Ballfield was dedicated to honor her contribution to girls' sports programs in the Village. (Pat Huson)

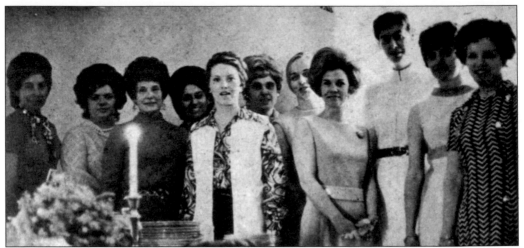

WOMEN'S CLUB. The Women's Club of Montgomery Village was founded in November 1968, and Kettler Brothers Inc. donated $100 to help in its organization. Peggy Kluge was the chair, and the organization helped raise money for many charities. The club sponsored the Children's Hospital Bridge Marathon, which annually raises money for Children's Hospital. The club relied mainly on luncheons, fashion shows, raffles, casino nights, bazaars, and skate, ski, and boot sales. One of the events raised funds to purchase a pulmonary resuscitator for the fire department. Money was also raised for local schools, hospitals, and scholarships. Social activities included New Year's Eve dances, a luau, an Oktoberfest, a square dance, a Fifties dance, bridge luncheons, wine and cheese parties, and various tours. Maryland representative Gilbert Gude and his wife, Jane, hosted the women on a tour of the Capitol in November 1971. (Peggy Kluge.)

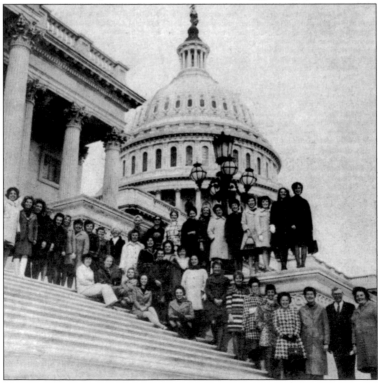

The Legend of General Digging. In 1966, while planning the Whetstone community, Kettler Brothers Inc. obtained the diary of Roger Brooke Farquar, written during the 1800s. It was decided to name all the streets in Whetstone alphabetically, based on actual historical entries from the diary. However, when it came to finding a name beginning with the letter "D," the developers were stumped. According to Bill Hurley, the curious name of "Digging Way" came about after someone read in the diary about a day spent "digging post holes in the meadow." Early Digging Way residents, not pleased with this derivation, created a legendary figure, Gen. Charles C. Digging, of whom they could be proud. The General Digging Society dedicated a commemorative plaque on their street to celebrate the "little known" Confederate general who, following the battle of Gettysburg, rested overnight in a cornfield in what is now Montgomery Village. (Right, drawing by William S. Farr; below, John Umbarger.)

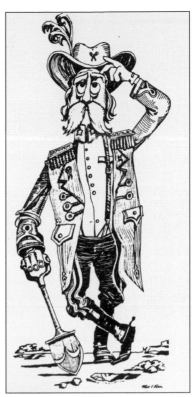

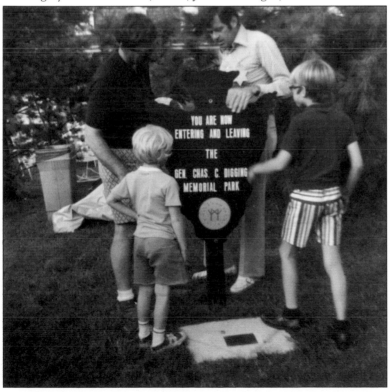

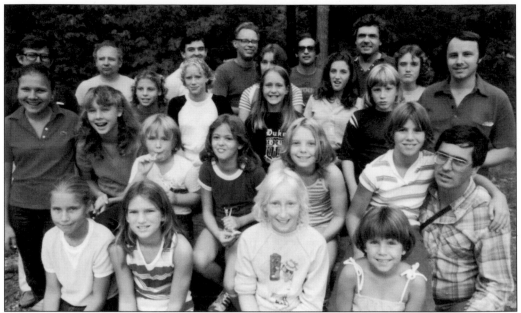

YOUTH ORGANIZATIONS. Scouting for both girls and boys and the YMCA Indian Guides and Princesses programs were popular family activities that provided an opportunity for early residents to get to know each other and participate in community activities. The Boy Scouts earned badges and engaged in service activities such as selling tickets for community events, picking up trash, and weeding around Lake Whetstone. Leadership, teamwork, and service were important values. The Girl Scouts enjoyed camping trips, musical shows, and earning badges. Indian Guides and Princesses attended meetings and camping trips, often searching for arrowheads, boating, swimming, and having fun with their fathers and friends. Leaders such as Neil Munch, George Arnold, and Rita Selman took the early initiative to engage and attract residents to these programs. (Above, Joe Maher; below, Dr. Elizabeth Arnold.)

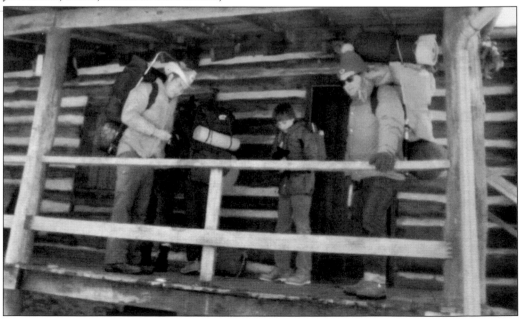

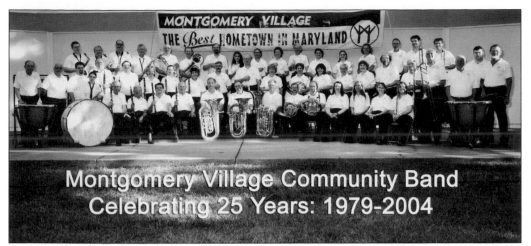

Montgomery Village Community Band
Celebrating 25 Years: 1979-2004

THE MONTGOMERY VILLAGE COMMUNITY BAND. The Montgomery Village Community Band (MVCB), established in 1979, is a nonprofit, all-volunteer organization sponsored by the MVF. The concert band has earned an excellent reputation for providing quality musical entertainment and is considered one of the premier community bands in Maryland. It has steadily grown from a dozen players to a well-balanced concert band that is over 70 players strong. During that time, several hundred different musicians have enjoyed the fun and satisfaction of playing concert band music with the MVCB. (Jocelyn Weinberg.)

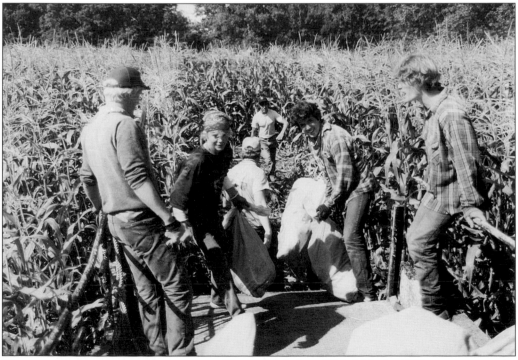

HOMEGROWN SUCCESS FOR MONTGOMERY VILLAGE. Mark and Eric Moholt of Whetstone started a farm stand business in 1978. They borrowed $5,000 from their father, Pete, and hired a farmer to plant and fertilize a crop of Silver Queen corn on 40 acres of rented land. They hired friends and family to pick the corn and sold it at stands nearby. Many Village teens worked on the summer corn projects from 1978 to 1983. (Pete Moholt.)

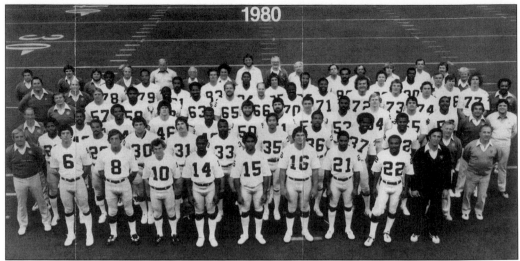

PHIL LIVINGSTON, OAKLAND RAIDERS NO. 76, 1980. Livingston (fourth row, third from right) achieved acclaim both in academics and athletics. He played on many MVSA teams and played football for Gaithersburg High School, the University of Maryland, and the Oakland Raiders. While at Maryland, he was the first recipient of the M Club Founders Award for outstanding athletic ability, academic excellence, honorable character, and notable citizenship, and he earned All-ACC academic honors. (Phil Livingston.)

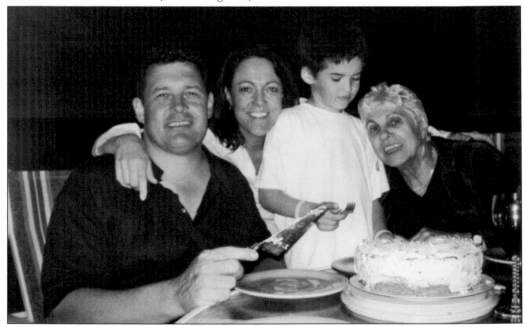

TOM McHALE, PROFESSIONAL FOOTBALL PLAYER. McHale played football for the MVSA and then at Gaithersburg High School. He received a scholarship to the University of Maryland but ended up at Cornell University's School of Hotel Administration. He then began a nine-year career in the National Football League, first with the Tampa Bay Buccaneers, then the Philadelphia Eagles, and finally with the Miami Dolphins. Before his NFL success, Tom worked for the Moholt corn-picking business. He is seen here with, from left, his sister, Margy McHale, his son Michael, and his mother, Joan McHale. (Margy McHale.)

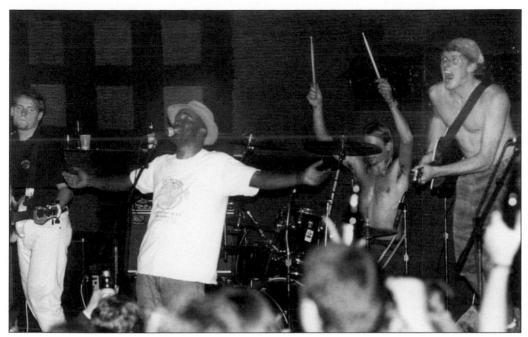

MARK BRYAN, LEAD GUITARIST, HOOTIE AND THE BLOWFISH. Bryan grew up in Fairway Island and is a cofounder and lead guitarist for the world-famous rock band Hootie and the Blowfish. His Village band, the Norms, played at the Lawn Theater in the summer of 1988. Mark also worked in the cornfields for the Moholt brothers. Before Hootie and the Blowfish hit it big, Mark was still cutting grass for the MVF in the summer months. (Mark Bryan.)

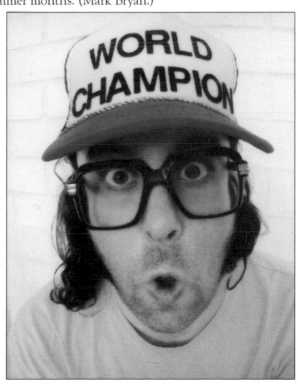

JUDAH FRIEDLANDER, COMEDIAN. Before ever becoming "The World Champion" in his stand-up act, a nominated and award-winning actor, or writer Frank Rossitano on NBC's megahit *30 Rock*, Friedlander was just a kid from Whetstone who excelled as a student, musician, and athlete. Today, he is an internationally acclaimed comedian of stage and screen. Some of his credits include *Meet the Parents, Zoolander, The Wrestler, 30 Rock, Curb Your Enthusiasm*, and "the Hug Guy" in the Dave Matthews Band's "Everyday" music video. (Shirley Friedlander.)

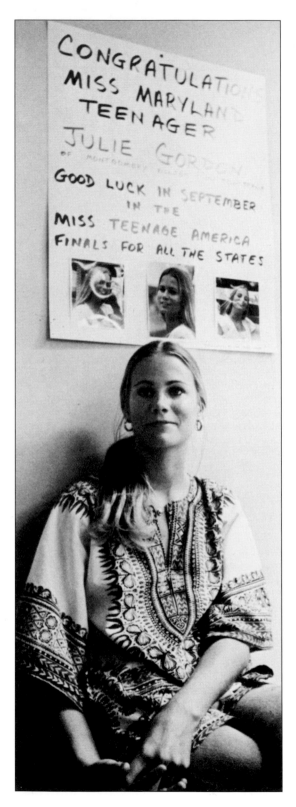

JULIE GORDON. After winning the Miss Maryland Teenager competition, Gordon completed her senior year at Gaithersburg High School. She went on to a successful 15-year career with the Ford Modeling Agency. In her career, she has been in national network television commercials and also had parts in several feature films and popular soap operas. She is now designing the "Yes Dress" and is cofounder of Between the Chicks.

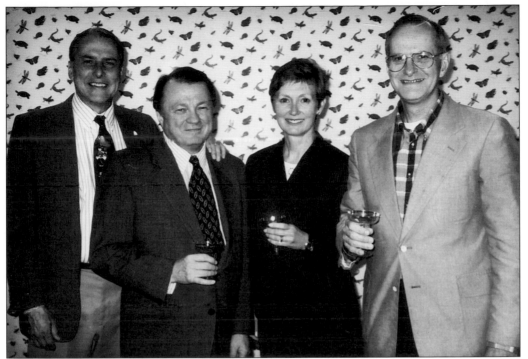

PEDIATRICIANS. Opening their pediatric practice in 1970, Drs. Frank Pedreira, Gordon Mella, and Edward Feroli were the first physicians at the Montgomery Village Professional Center. Dr. Pedreira, who lives in Whetstone, is still a member of the practice. In June 1998, the group became affiliated with the Children's National Medical Center and changed its name to Children's Pediatricians. Village families have always felt confident knowing competent pediatric care is minutes from home. (Frank Pedreira.)

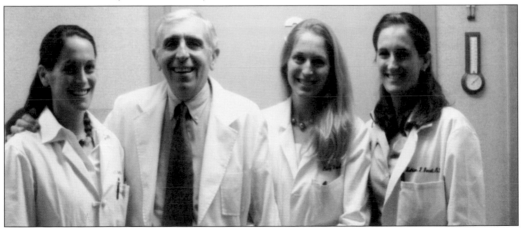

THE DOCTORS FREKKO. In 1971, Dr. Tibor Frekko fulfilled the need of Kettler Brothers Inc. for a family doctor in the new Professional Center. For the Frekkos, that was the start of a wonderful journey into Village life. Office visits were $7, he made many house calls, and he had Saturday and weekend hours. Early patients included up-county farmers and the occasional celebrity, such as the singing group the Temptations. Dr. Frekko's three daughters—Drs. Ann Frekko Raffo (left), Mary Frekko (center), and Kathleen Frekko Farrell—all became physicians and have joined this true family practice. (Truda Frekko.)

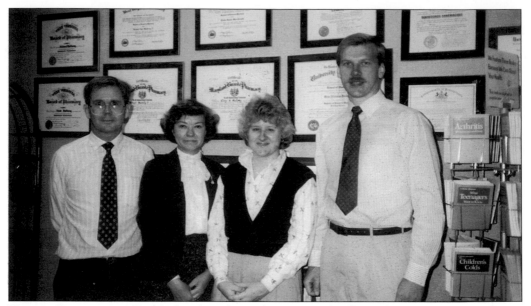

VILLAGE PHARMACIST. Richard and Linda Matheny opened Village Pharmacist Inc. in 1973 in the Professional Center. Offering a new concept—"a professional pharmacy with no signage, no visible merchandise, free delivery, ample consultation, and 24-hour emergency service"—they attempted to recreate the corner drugstore. Expanding their space and staff enabled them to service a greater need. Today, the pharmacy remains open, and these same four pharmacists still serve the Village. From left are Richard and Linda Matheny, Judy Allison, and Gene Borowski. (Richard Matheny.)

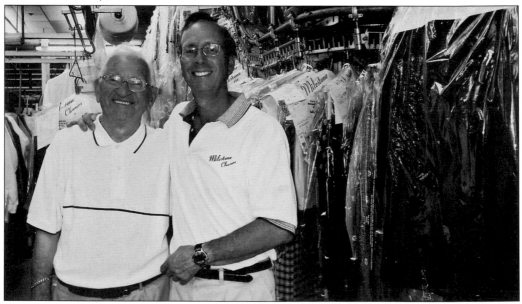

ZACHARY (LEFT) AND RONNIE GREENBAUM. Zachary Greenbaum owned a dry cleaner in the early 1950s in the Friendship Heights area of Washington, DC. In the mid-1960s, one of his regular customers, Clarence Kettler, asked if Greenbaum would like to open a shop in the new town he was building near Gaithersburg, Maryland. Greenbaum opened his new store in October 1970 and remained close friends and business partners with Clarence Kettler. (Ronnie Greenbaum.)

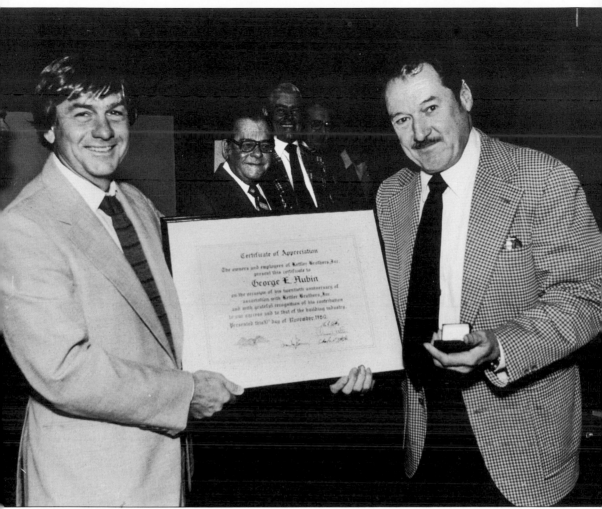

CLARENCE KETTLER AND GEORGE AUBIN, 1980. In 1960, architect George Aubin (right) was hired by Kettler Brothers Inc. as its service manager, and he was promoted to vice president in charge of special projects during the development of Montgomery Village. Aubin designed the golf course building, some rental townhouses and apartments, and several shops in the Village Mall. When the original hardware store went out of business, the Aubins took over the shop, turning it into a successful enterprise. Aubin's wife, Patricia, sold wallpaper, antiques, furniture, and dollhouse furniture to many Village residents. In the mid-1980s, after Patricia finished a degree in education, they designed and built the Village Montessori School. Today, their three daughters run the school, Patricia is semi-retired, and George likes to joke that he's still the head of the maintenance division. (George Aubin.)

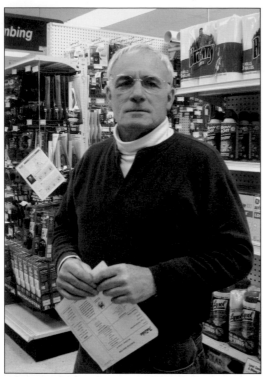

VAN SCHENCK. Kettler Brothers Inc. sold the hardware store to the Schenck family in 1980. From the beginning, the mantra at Schenck's was customer service, offering advice as well as hardware. For help with home projects, Schenck not only told customers how but also loaned the tools needed. Whether it was a specific paint color or an extra key, residents could find it, along with a friendly smile, at Schenck's. Sadly, the store closed in 2010.

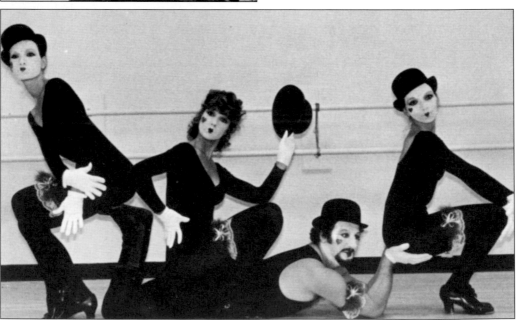

MONTGOMERY VILLAGE CENTER FOR THE PERFORMING ARTS. With the support of Clarence Kettler, Carol and Bob Dendall founded the Center for the Performing Arts in 1974. Starting with 12 students, the school grew to more than 500 students by 1977. In 1980, when the Dendalls moved to California, Sherry Witt took over their dream. The center offered a variety of classes in the arts. When the Village Mall was remodeled in 1989, the Center for the Performing Arts was forced to close its doors. (Sherry Witt.)

Seven

PROGRAMS AND EVENTS

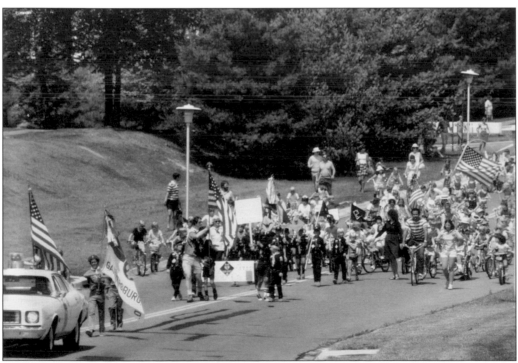

FOURTH OF JULY PARADE ALONG WATKINS MILL ROAD. "You don't have to travel to have fun" was the Kettler brothers' original slogan for the annual Fourth of July celebration, but it could serve as the year-round, year-in and year-out motto for all the programs available in the Village. From special events to classes and camps, clubs and organizations to committees and boards, and playgrounds to senior activities, there is something for everyone and for all ages all year long.

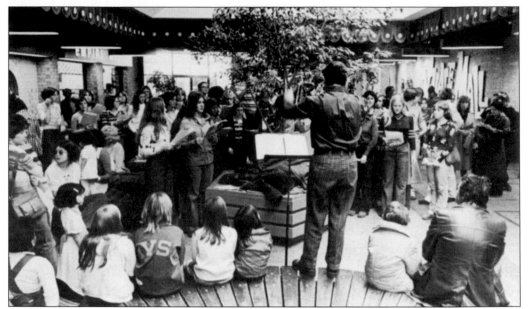

VILLAGE MALL SPECIAL EVENTS, 1971–1972. When the Village Mall first opened in 1970, the Merchants' Association of Montgomery Village Shopping Mall was formed, with officers elected among the mall's business owners. This organization sponsored many special events, including dances, concerts, art shows, an antique show, an international festival, a summer camping show, fashion shows, auctions, and more. Kettler Brothers Inc. also sponsored several special events, including an annual photography contest put on display at the visitor's center.

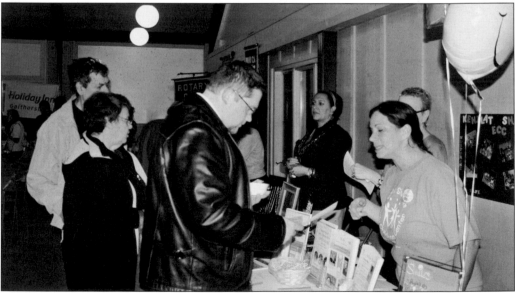

NEW RESIDENT WELCOME RECEPTION, 2009. In early years, a visitor's center welcomed prospective and new residents. There, they could find information about the amenities in the Village as well as the responsibilities of owners in a planned community with architectural standards and covenants. In recent years, the MVF hosts an annual Welcome Reception where local businesses, doctors, dentists, elected officials, and foundation staff meet with new residents to answer questions and provide useful information.

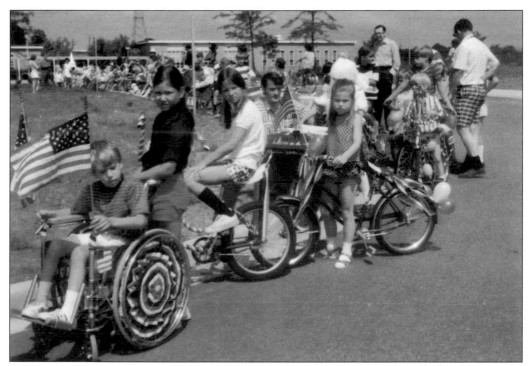

FOURTH OF JULY CELEBRATION, 1972 AND 2006. From the beginning, Independence Day was an occasion for a Village-wide celebration, including a parade, with prizes in different categories of decorated bikes, trikes, and floats, games, and entertainment for the whole family. Swim teams and foundation camps are perennial participants. This annual celebration was first held in 1969 at Whetstone Community Center and pool, the only center built at that time, with activities that included a cookout, bingo, and swim meets followed by an evening fireworks display from the Lake Whetstone island jointly sponsored by the Gaithersburg Recreation Department and Montgomery Village. Later, the celebration was moved to South Valley Park and included all-star baseball games, a midway, and a 5K cross-country run. The fireworks display was moved to the Gaithersburg fairgrounds in 1981, when construction began on the Dockside townhome community adjacent to Lake Whetstone. (Above, Kari Salmonsen; below, MVF.)

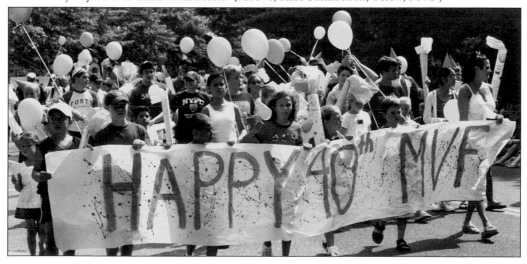

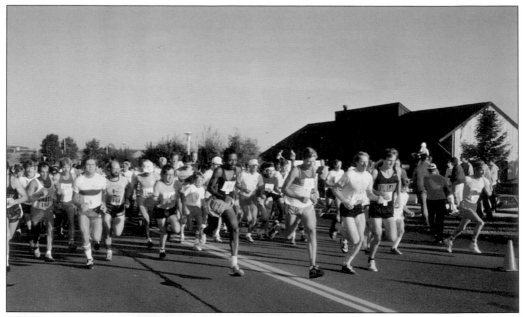

10K Race from North Creek, 1988. For several years, an annual 10K race called "Life, Be In It" was held in the fall, jointly sponsored by the MVF and the City of Gaithersburg. Beginning in 1990, this was replaced by an early-morning 5K cross-country race along with a one-mile fun walk incorporated into the annual MVF Fourth of July festivities. Ribbons are awarded in different age categories for men, women, boys, and girls, and whole families often participate.

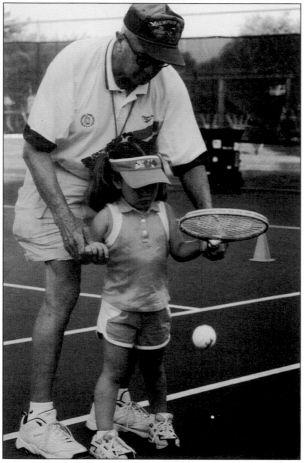

Tennis Instructor Ski Aller, 2006. With over 25 courts located throughout the Village, tennis has always been a popular activity for residents of all ages. In addition to classes for adults and youth, men's, women's, and seniors' clubs meet regularly for competitive play. For years, tennis ladders were a Village staple. Over the years, the foundation has offered advanced tennis clinics, a tennis carnival, a tennis camp, and even winter indoor "QuickStart" classes for young children in the Lake Marion gymnasium.

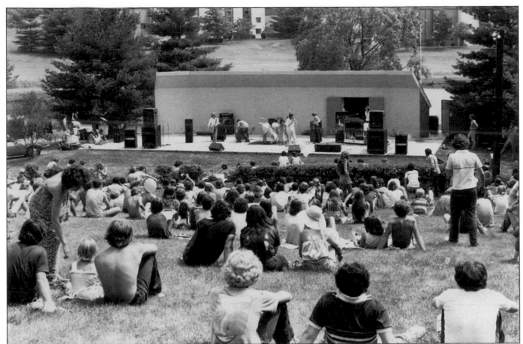

MVF Lawn Theater. Providing the venue for a Sunday evening summer concert series featuring an eclectic assortment of entertainers, the natural amphitheater in South Valley Park, known as the Lawn Theater, opened in August 1968. Concertgoers are encouraged to bring the whole family, pack a picnic dinner, blankets or lawn chairs, and enjoy the music in the open air. The relaxed atmosphere has some in the audience reclining on blankets, while others are moved to jump up and dance to the beat. The original Lawn Theater structure was remodeled in 2009 with the help of a matching state grant and now offers a covered venue with enhanced acoustics.

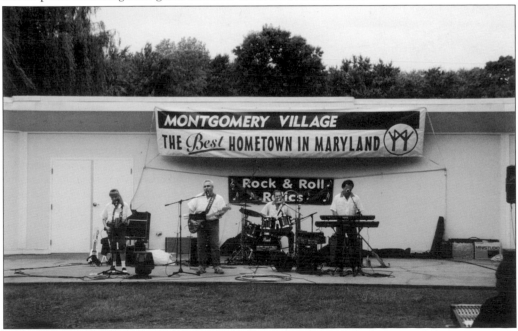

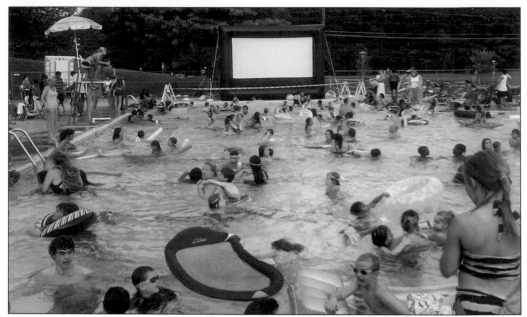

DIVE-IN MOVIE, 2010. Held at dusk at Stedwick Pool, the only pool in the Village that is lit at night, the Dive-In Movie has always been a popular summer event. Participants are permitted to bring rafts, which are not normally allowed in the pools during regular hours. A child-appropriate movie is shown on a big screen, while the audience may watch from the water or poolside.

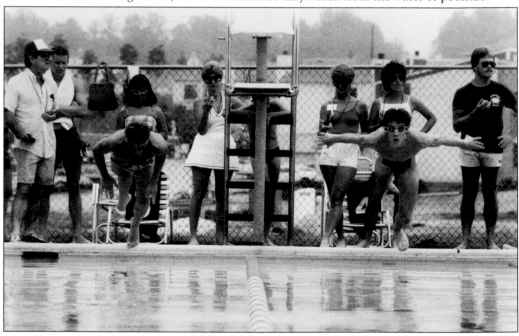

ALL-COMERS SWIM MEET. The first Montgomery Village Open Swimming Meet was held in 1974, and it has since been held in early June every year. Swimmers ages six to 18 can compete "just for the fun of it," whether they swim regularly with one of the Village swim teams or not. In each event, awards are given to first through 12th place for ages six to 12 and first through sixth place for ages 13 to 18.

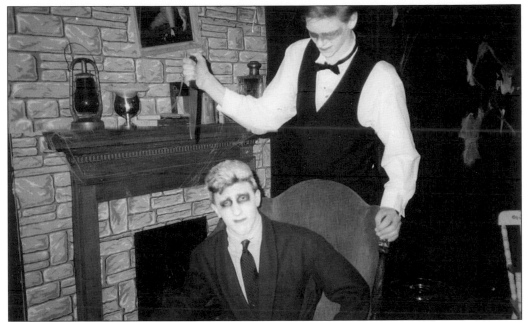

HAUNTED HOUSE, 1989. Once a year, a haunted house, unlike any of the designs of Kettler Brothers Inc. and quite unfit for habitation, sprang up in the Village in time for Halloween visits. Appearing first in the North Creek Community Center garage, then for some years in a Village Mall storefront, where the event was cosponsored by Montgomery County Recreation Department, the annual project was eventually ended due to the heavy construction demands plus fire and safety concerns.

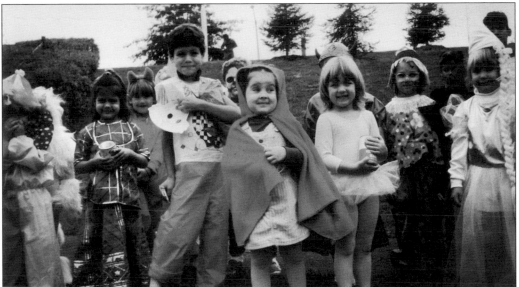

HALLOWEEN SPOOKTACULAR. This annual event for children ages three to nine features a costume parade and contest, crafts, spooky music, games, and a fortune-teller. Donations of nonperishable food items are requested, to be delivered to a local food bank. Story and poster contests are also held in partnership with the local elementary schools. Ribbons are awarded to first through third place in each age category, with winning stories printed in the *Montgomery Village News*.

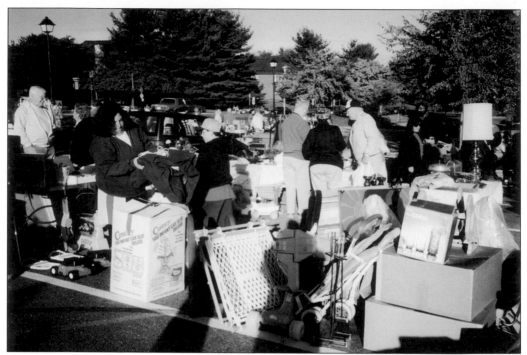

FALL FLEA MARKET, 1994. This popular event, held in both spring and fall each year, draws crowds of bargain hunters seeking treasures among others' discards. Food and beverages are also sold as fundraisers for Scouts and swim teams.

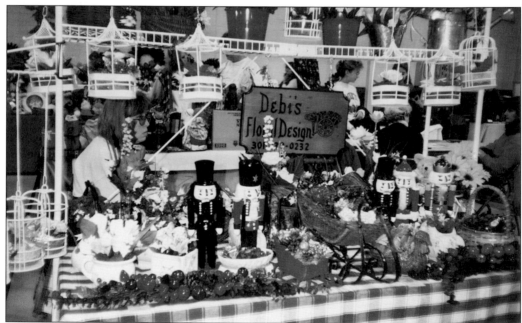

HOLIDAY CRAFT BAZAAR. This annual event offers handmade crafts of all kinds, including jewelry, Christmas ornaments, art objects, and creative collectors' items for sale just in time for the holidays. Festive music welcomes crowds of shoppers, who stop on their way out to purchase homemade goodies from the local Girl Scouts.

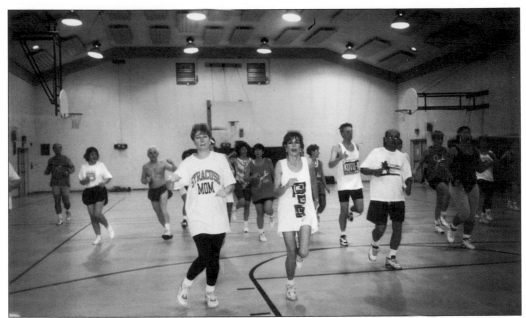

THANKSGIVING MORNING AEROBIC SAMPLER, 2000. When Lake Marion, the newest of the four Village community centers, opened in 1988 with both an activity room and a gymnasium, most exercise programs, indoor sports, and off-season team practices were moved to the gym. In 1994, aerobics instructor Karin Baker, on the right in the image at right with Nancy Brouillette, and co-instructors held the first Thanksgiving Morning Aerobic Sampler, with the slogan "Work up a Hunger to Feed the Hungry" setting the tone of the workout. Participants bring donations of canned food and/or cash, all of which is donated to local charities. Every year since, this spirited annual tradition continues to attract students, their families, and friends. The recent economic downturn has brought forth other grassroots donations, including Food for Schools and Coats for Kids.

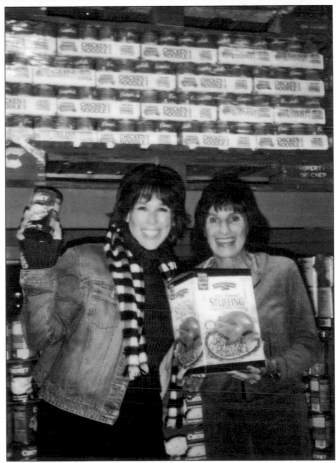

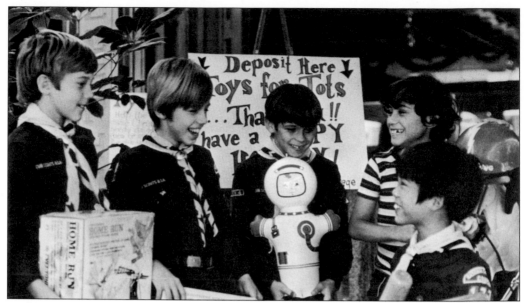

CUB SCOUTS, 1972. Many Village organizations, in addition to the MVF, have focused their efforts through the years on charitable initiatives. These include the Scouts, Woman's Club, Rotary, Kiwanis, and other local clubs. Pictured here are Cub Scouts collecting donations for the US Marines Toys for Tots Foundation, which also benefits from donations at the annual MVCB Christmas Concert.

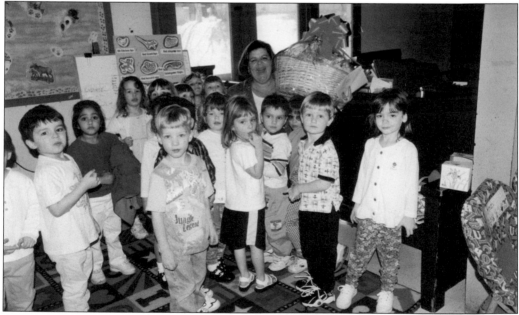

CREATIVE PLAYTIME CELEBRATING 25 YEARS, MARCH 2000. In 1975, the MVF began offering its own preschool program under Kathi Hufnagel's instruction. This replaced Montgomery County's Creative Carousel program, which had been held in the MVF's community centers. Many Village three- and four-year-olds have begun their love of learning in Hufnagel's capable hands, exploring the excitement of music, drama, movement, crafts, nature, and playtime, as well as developing the cognitive, physical, and social skills essential to kindergarten success.

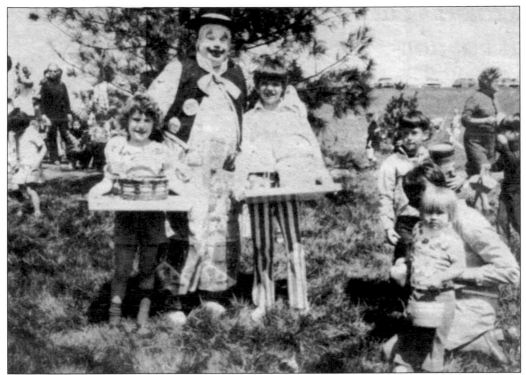

EASTER EGG HUNT, APRIL 12, 1971. Originally, the annual Easter Egg hunt was jointly sponsored by the Montgomery Village Women's Club and the MVF and held on the slopes of the Lawn Theatre in South Valley Park. This well-attended event included prizes, candy, Easter eggs, and a troop of festive clowns.

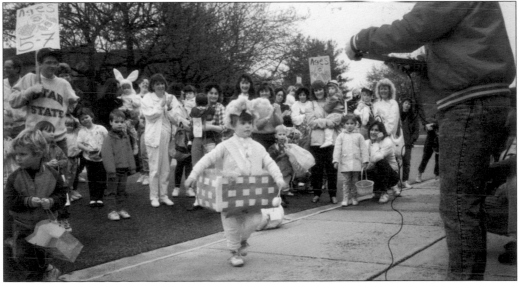

SPRING FROLIC, APRIL 1992. The annual Easter-themed event continued to be a popular spring children's event as part of the MVF's programming. The Spring Frolic was held at one of the Village community centers, with outdoor activities (weather permitting), games, costume contests, and more.

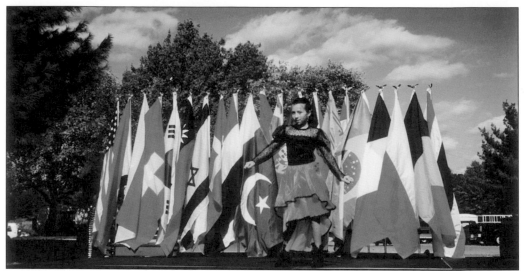

INTERNATIONAL FESTIVAL, 1995. Fall in the Village has always been celebrated with a festival of some kind, including food, music, crafts, and other entertainment. In the early years, Kettler Brothers Inc. and Village Mall merchants provided the venue, celebrating with an Oktoberfest theme. The MVF continued that motif for many years, but as the community evolved and interests changed, other concepts were introduced—the Americana Festival and for several years the International Festival, among others—often in partnership with Village schools.

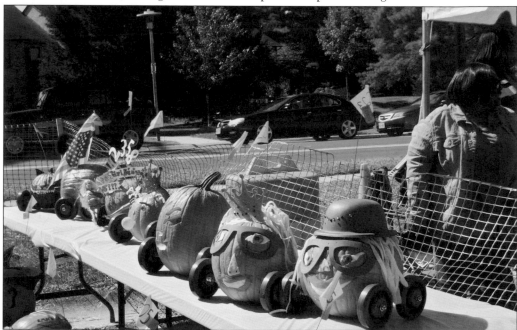

FALL FESTIVAL AND GREAT PUMPKIN RACES, OCTOBER, 2010. The annual MVF Fall Festival took on a new look in 2010, when the major focus was on participants who entered their decorated pumpkin racing cars to compete against each other for rewards. Prizes were also awarded in several categories for best-decorated pumpkin. This fun event, held at North Creek Community Center, was accompanied by live music, food, scarecrow making, hayrides, games, and crafts. (Roslyn Price.)

PLANTING THE VILLAGE CHRISTMAS TREE, 1995. Early Village residents felt a strong sense of community and came together with enthusiasm at every opportunity to celebrate. For several years, a small community Christmas tree was decorated for the holidays in the space between the original visitor center and the Aquatic Center, which became the YMCA. Residents had punch and cookies and sang carols. That tree came down when the Village Mall was remodeled into an outdoor strip mall. But in 1995, a new tree was planted adjacent to the mall along Montgomery Village Avenue. Every year since, the MVF has held a tree-lighting ceremony, with an appearance by Santa, hot chocolate, an ensemble of the MVCB, and the Watkins Mill High School Chamber Singers to welcome in the holiday season.

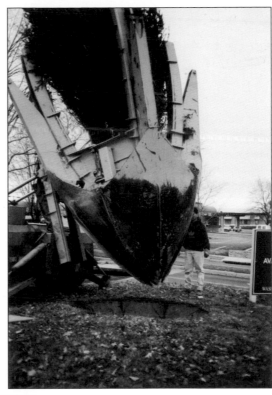

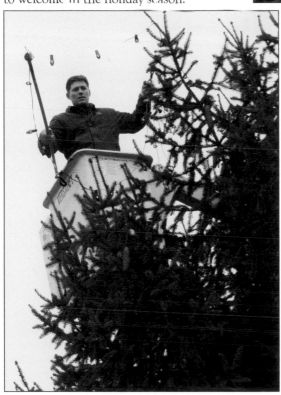

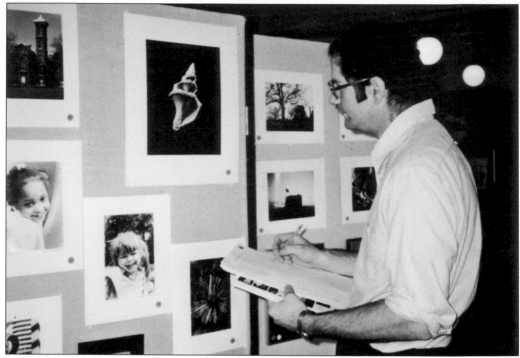

ANNUAL ART SHOW, 1988. The Art, Craft, and Photography Show was originally sponsored by Doug Brown of the Village Framer and held in the Village Mall. Beginning in 1975, the show became one of the MVF's annual special events. Each year in early March, this juried show is held in North Creek Community Center and judged by members of the local fine arts club, who award ribbons in various age and media categories.

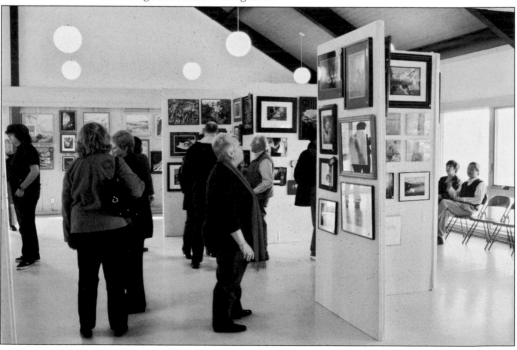

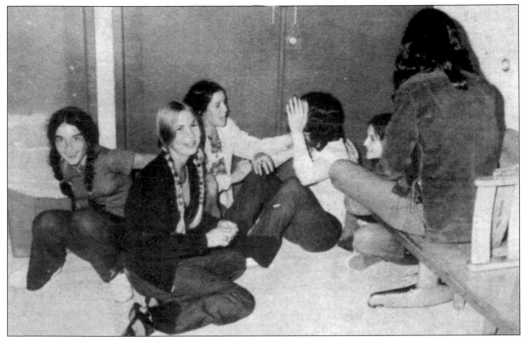

TEEN CLUB, 1972. This early Teen Club met Friday and Saturday nights at Stedwick Community Center. The MVF continued to work hard to address the after-school needs of preteens and teens when the Youth of the 90s Club was formed with the help of a county grant to accommodate primarily middle school teens who could easily walk to Stedwick from school. More recently, the Teen Center meets on Friday nights for games, movies, special events, and refreshments.

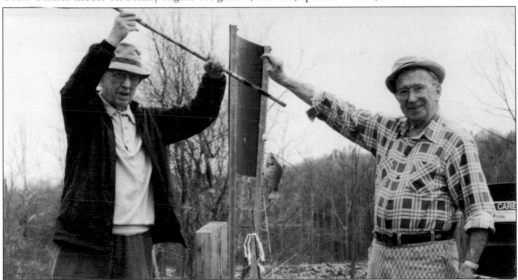

GOOD OL' BOYS FISHING TRIP, 1986. Senior men and women originally met separately. Senior men (self-named the "Good Ol' Boys") met at North Creek for cards, pool, and other games. The women's group, sponsored by Montgomery County, met at Walker House for crafts and other activities. When the county moved its funding, the ladies' program joined the City of Gaithersburg senior program. As the Village has aged, so have many of its residents, resulting in renewed interest in providing coed senior programming.

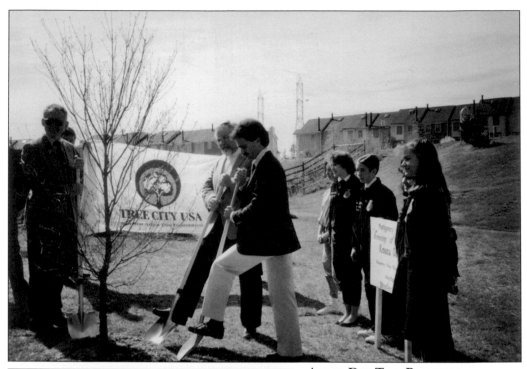

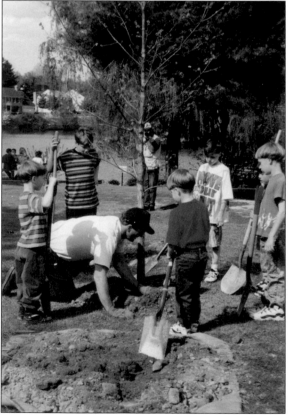

ARBOR DAY TREE PLANTING. Protecting and preserving wherever practicable healthy, growing trees, Kettler Brothers Inc. was careful to take maximum advantage of the natural beauty of the area. Since so much of the original land had been farmed, it was also necessary to plant a great many trees. The MVF has conscientiously maintained this tradition, and each year, the landscaping department plants new trees to replace those that have succumbed to the attrition of time or disease. As a result, the MVF has been recognized for 22 consecutive years by the Arbor Day Foundation for honoring its commitment to community forestry. The Tree City USA program, sponsored by the Arbor Day Foundation in cooperation with the National Association of State Foresters and the USDA Forest Service, found that Montgomery Village met its standards to receive this honor.

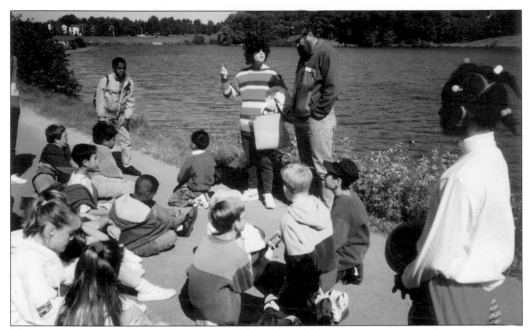

NATURE PROGRAM AT LAKE WHETSTONE, 1993. Protecting the natural environment was a priority for the developers and continues to be an integral part of Village life. The MVF has worked hard over the years to involve youngsters in environmental education, including protection of and coexistence with wildlife, cleaning park areas, and keeping the Village green. Here, natural resources specialist Mark Swick conducts a program for elementary school children at Lake Whetstone.

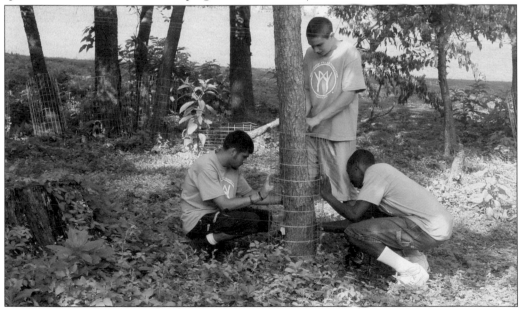

YOUTH CORPS WRAPPING TREES, 2004. The Youth Corps is an MVF paid summer program for teens 14 and older working under adult supervision to complete park and environmental projects. Here, they are working to wrap trees near lakes and ponds to protect them from hungry beavers. These youngsters assist with cleanup of park and stream areas, wetland planting, weeding, and other tasks to beautify the Village environment.

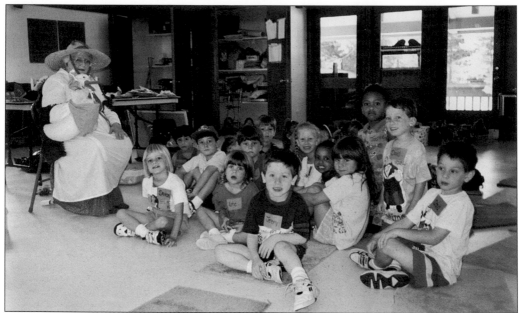

SUMMER CAMPS. The MVF offers four popular eight-week summer camps certified by the state of Maryland for ages ranging from preschoolers to teens. Each session is planned to accentuate a different theme and combines learning with indoor and outdoor fun, including swimming, crafts, special events, sports, swim lessons for the "Tiny Feet" campers, and field trips for the older participants. Camps meet at Village community centers and provide extended-care options. Through the years, specialty camps have also been offered, including band camps, tennis camps, and other sports camps. Supervised drop-in programs are available for those who prefer a less structured program.

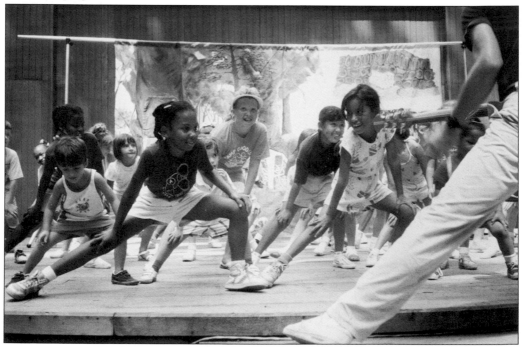

Eight

THE VILLAGE TODAY

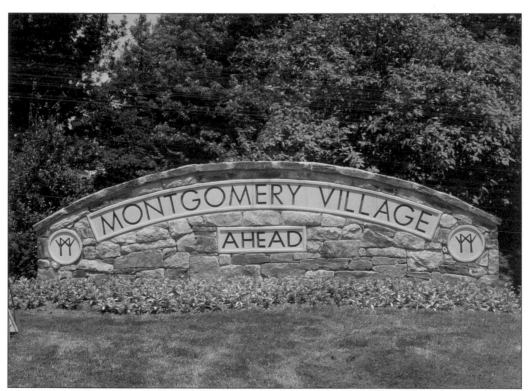

MONTGOMERY VILLAGE TODAY. In 2011, Montgomery Village has more than 40,000 residents living in a wide variety of residential facilities, offering a broad range of structural types, site-planning layouts, and rental and purchase prices. Villagers have access to recreational, commercial, and cultural facilities. Like the rest of Montgomery County, Montgomery Village is at a pivotal moment as it seeks to position itself for the next 50 years of land-use planning.

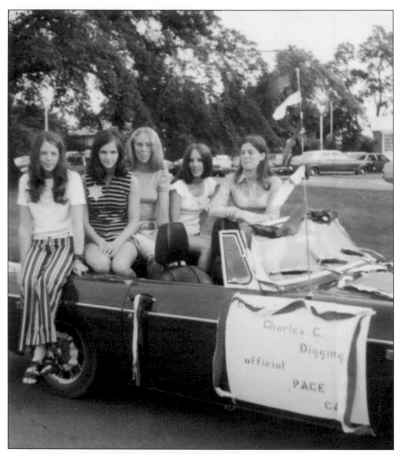

A Vision Realized. In the 1960s, Kettler Brothers Inc. had an innovative vision to create a planned community that provided a high quality of life in harmony with nature. This vision has been realized, and today, Montgomery Village mirrors the diversity and demographic change seen in the rest of Montgomery County. The change in the diversity of residents can be seen in the multicultural expansion of programs found in the community. (Left, John Umbarger; below, Dave Lechner.)

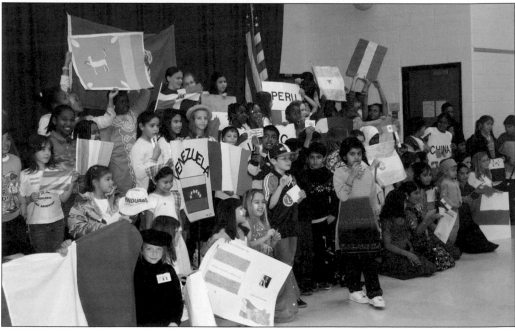

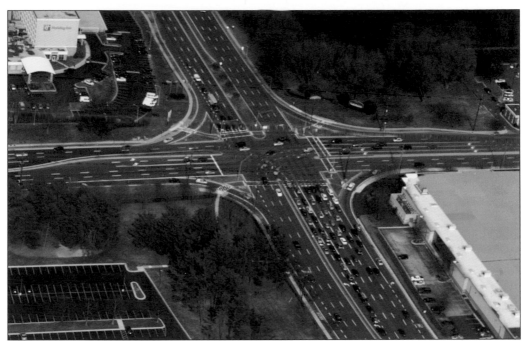

CONVENIENT TO A GROWING TRANSPORTATION NETWORK. Montgomery Village has easy access to bus, rail, and car transportation. It offers proximity to the Washington Metropolitan Area's transportation network via the employment corridor of Interstate 270, the InterCounty Connector (ICC)/Route 200, or by way of Midcounty Highway to the Shady Grove Metro station. The county's Ride On bus service has various routes through the Village and connects riders to the other modes of travel in the transportation system. Village residents can travel to Gaithersburg to access the Maryland Area Regional Commuter (MARC) trains' daily service to Washington, DC. (Above, Montgomery County Department of Public Works and Transportation; below, MVF.)

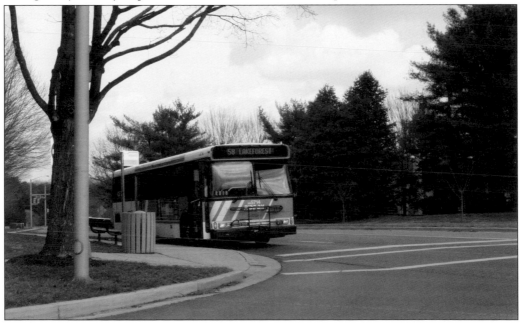

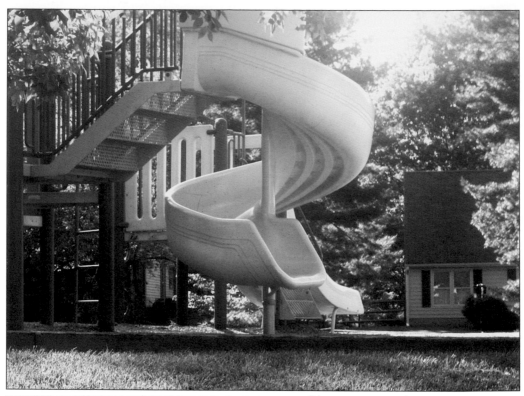

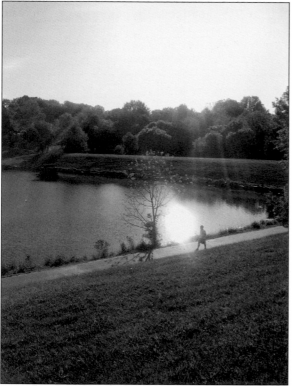

INCREASING THE AMOUNT OF COMMON AREA. The Montgomery Village Foundation has nurtured and sustained the growth of the Village and expanded its ownership of public land for the benefit of all residents. As members of the MVF, Village residents have access to the community infrastructure, including recreational facilities and more than 300 acres of green space with woods, streams, lakes, ponds, and meadow parkland. (Above, Joanne Miller; left, Blanca Sanchez.)

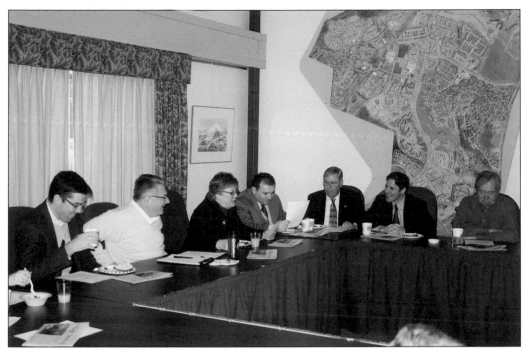

GOVERNING THE COMMUNITY. The Montgomery Village Foundation is a partnership of all its members, which include all Village homeowners dwelling in numerous homes corporations, condominium associations, and multifamily rental apartments. The MVF represents the community to the state and local governments. Shown here, each year the MVF Board of Directors hosts a meeting with state and county representatives to discuss mutual concerns and solutions. The MVF provides maintenance and administrative services to the local homes corporations as desired on a contractual basis. The policies of the foundation are determined by its elected board of directors. A full-time professional staff implements the programs and policies of the foundation.

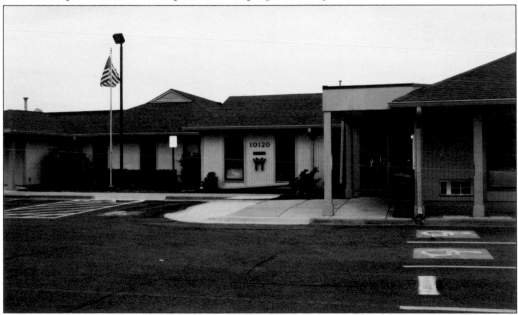

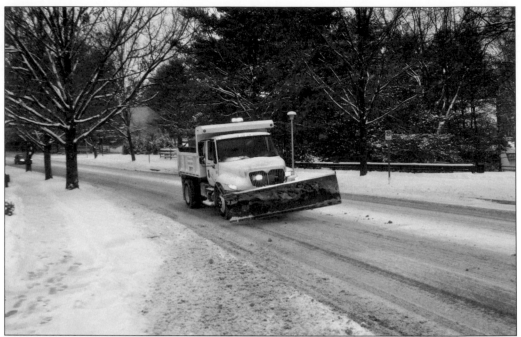

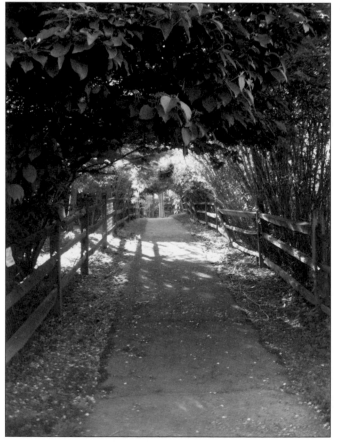

CARING FOR THE COMMUNITY. The homes corporations in the Village are owned and operated by residents through representative boards. The local homes corporation owns and maintains the streets and green spaces, provides common services such as trash collection, and develops and enforces maintenance standards for the homes. Homes corporations are funded by the members through their assessments. They are governed by resident-elected boards of directors that represent the community to the MVF, Montgomery County, and the State of Maryland. Residents and homeowners volunteer to serve on committees and provide feedback, comments, and information. One service valued by all residents is snow removal. (Above, MVF; left, Mariana Camacho.)

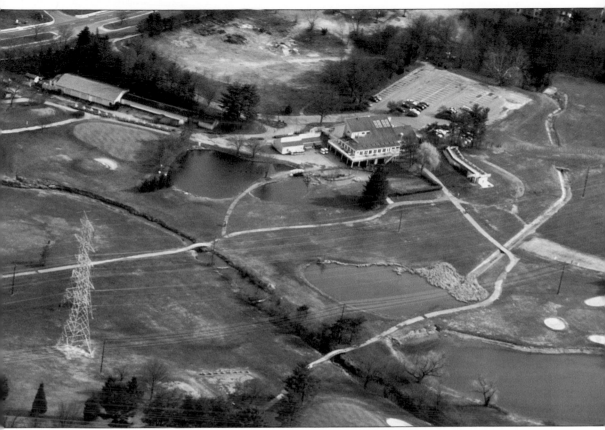

The Montgomery Village Golf Club. The Montgomery Village Golf Club has been an important feature of the community from the very beginning. While it is a private club, it offers benefits to the public such as dining and recreation services and seasonal scenic beauty, and it maintains and preserves the wetlands and provides a buffer between the high-voltage power lines and the surrounding community. Facing declining membership in recent years, the golf course is one of four properties in the Village identified for potential redevelopment. An agreement has been reached with a developer who would like to incorporate some residential development while keeping some open space. (Montgomery County Department of Public Works and Transportation.)

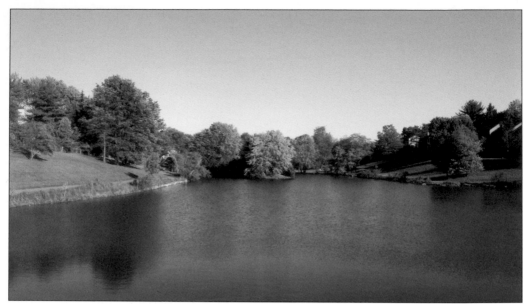

CONTINUING FOCUS ON THE ENVIRONMENT. The original plan of Montgomery Village addressed the need for environmental stewardship with economic benefits. Open spaces and recreational areas are situated to integrate individual communities. Lake Whetstone is a scenic and recreational amenity and provides storm water management for parts of the Village and Gaithersburg, benefiting Seneca Creek, the Potomac River, and the Chesapeake Bay. In recognition of this, Montgomery County has agreed to maintain Lake Whetstone, including erosion and sediment control. (Above, Mariana Camacho; below, Roslyn Price.)

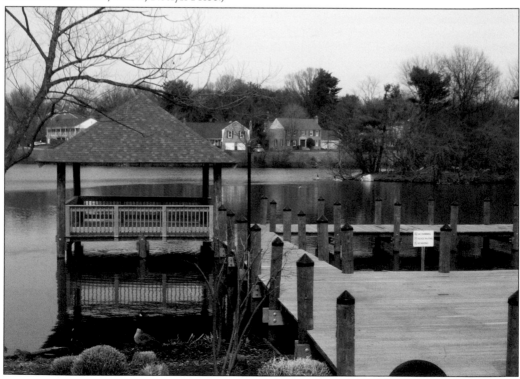

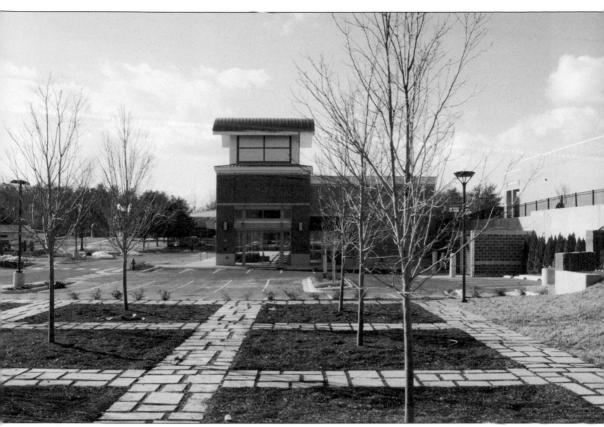

NEW COMMERCIAL CENTERS. Montgomery Village provides convenient access to commercial and professional services. The newest addition to the shopping options in Montgomery Village will be the Marketplace (opening in 2011), seen here on the former site of the YMCA. Over the years, the commercial area in the town center of the Village has seen many changes, and today it is a primary focus of future land-use planning. (Joanne Miller.)

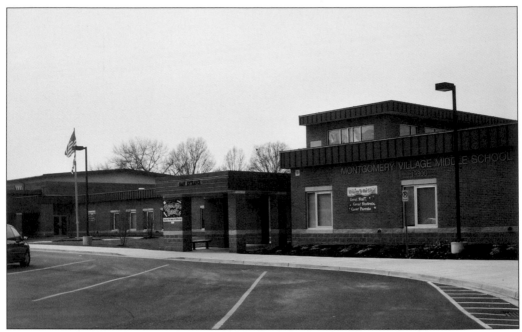

EDUCATIONAL OPTIONS AVAILABLE. Today, students in Montgomery Village have access to public and private education. The two public high schools, Gaithersburg and Watkins Mill, and the seven feeder elementary and five feeder middle schools in the Montgomery County Public School system serve the children of the Village. Village residents have convenient access to two-year and four-year higher education opportunities as well as adult education at Montgomery College's Germantown and Rockville campuses and the Universities at Shady Grove. Montgomery Village Middle School was renovated in 2003, and Whetstone Elementary, the first school opened in the Village, is also in the midst of renovations. (Above, Roslyn Price; below, Joanne Miller.)

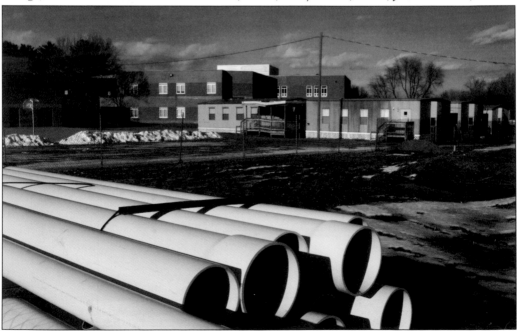

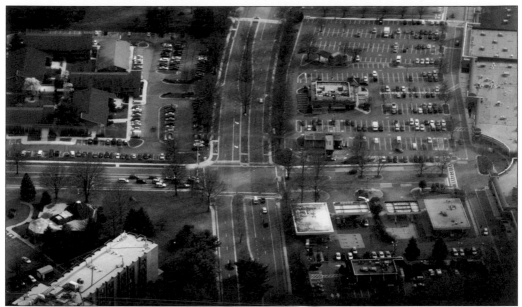

CREATING A VISION FOR THE FUTURE. Today, the Montgomery Village Foundation's strategic plan, called Vision 2030, focuses on the future land use in and around the growing community. In 2011, the MVF invited local and national planning experts and officials to share trends in community planning and is reaching out to all Village stakeholders to encourage their awareness and participation in this vision for the future of the Village. The main areas of focus include the commercial areas of the Montgomery Village Center, the Professional Center, the golf course, and the entrance parcel at Montgomery Village Avenue and Lost Knife Road. This effort is closely aligned with the expected updating of the Town Sector Zoning Ordinance, which governs development in Montgomery Village, and the updating of the Gaithersburg East Master Plan. Both of these are on schedule to be revised about 2014. (Both, Montgomery County Department of Public Works and Transportation.)

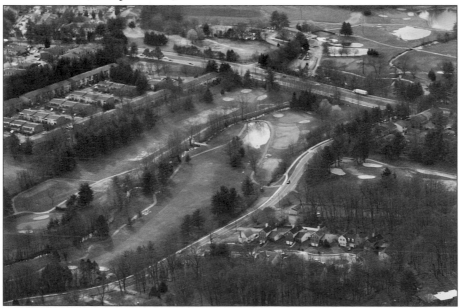

www.arcadiapublishing.com

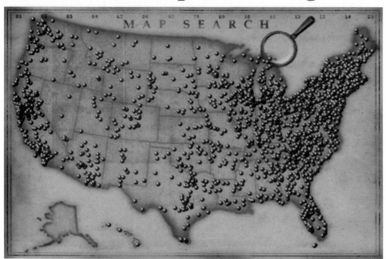

Discover books about the town where you grew up, the cities where your friends and families live, the town where your parents met, or even that retirement spot you've been dreaming about. Our Web site provides history lovers with exclusive deals, advanced notification about new titles, e-mail alerts of author events, and much more.

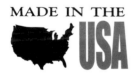

Find Your Place in History.